DATE DUE	RETURNED

DISCARD

Screenplay and Essays on the Film

Derrida

Kirby Dick and Amy Ziering Kofman DIRECTORS

Foreword by Geoffrey Hartman

Published in the United States and Canada in 2005 by
Routledge
270 Madison Avenue
New York, NY 10016
www.routledge-ny.com

Routledge is an imprint of the Taylor & Francis Group.

Copyright © 2005 by Jane Doe Films

Book design by Marika van Adelsberg / Los Angeles
Printed by Dual Graphics, Brea, California
Binding by Roswell Bookbinding
Printed on McCoy

ISBN   0 415 97408 9

Catalog Record is available from the Library of Congress.

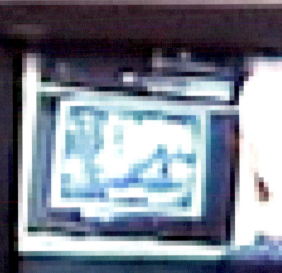

Screenplay and Essays on the Film

Derrida

Foreword by Geoffrey Hartman

Essays by Nicholas Royle, Kirby Dick

and Amy Ziering Kofman

Interviews with Jacques Derrida

Film to Text Adaptation by Gil Kofman

Contents

Foreword

Jacques Derrida, who had read the contents of this book, died before he could make good on his wish to contribute a personal reflection. This book is based on the film, DERRIDA, which premiered at the Sundance Film festival in 2003 and subsequently played in theaters nationally and internationally. Both book and film are an unusual tribute. They allow us to look more closely into Derrida's mind as well as into the thoughts of those who produced the film. It was a happy idea to make the script available in this form and add striking stills from the movie. A happy idea now tinged by sadness at the passing of so remarkable and humane a thinker.

I find the entire relation of verbal and filmic intriguing: how Derrida's demeanor and impromptu responses go along with or deflect the interviewers, then how these glimpses of him at home or pursuing daily activities illuminate what may have passed us by in his written work. We are also apprized of the many individual decisions shaping an art form that is a collective enterprise. Derrida may have enjoyed the unpredictables involved, as well as the skill and always courteous chutzpah of Ziering Kofman as interviewer. There are additional commentaries (he had a liking for such "hors d'oeuvres") by readers, journalists, and filmmakers as they ponder a "non-confessional" yet highly revealing portrait.

So this book is not exclusively for academics and deep scholars. It deserves as popular a reception as the film itself. In both book and film the man we see lends himself and his thoughts to a kind of peripatetic touring or Grand Rounds. Meditative, and predominantly a writer, everything for him begins by being "impossible;" and so he resists the direct questions, uncertain how personal or else professionally philosophic his answers should be. If he appears to be distracted, looking for his house keys, for example, or complaining (in good humor) about being followed, it is because he conspires with the powerful yet potentially trivial focus of a camera enlisted to give deconstruction a human face. Deconstruction had become, in the popular American press, and even among some colleagues, a miscegenated monster: the Minotaur in the maze, waiting to entrap us by a fatal mixture of literary and philosophical, of verbalisms endlessly caught in the impasse of skeptical thought.

Yet here, surprisingly, although it should not surprise, since at least from the time of *Glas* (1974) Derrida had interwoven biographical and professional themes, the moving image of the man before us allows the realism of daily life to enter. He responds clearly to a challenge that inter-illuminates life and letters. "Qui, lui?" he had asked about Hegel at the beginning of *Glas*, "who, he?" Who is a philosopher, and who, what, is the "I" that can say "I"?

Already near the beginning of the film Derrida is shown lecturing on what a biography should entail, given its often lasting impact on reputation. He realizes that this movie about him is an image-making venture, though in his eyes less legitimate than reading closely even a single passage from the author being filmed. In this way the philosopher as movie-object, as Franco-American idol, enjoys the imaging game to which he is submitting with a genial reserve of irony.

How do you sum up the life of a person who is also a philosopher? Derrida questions

Heidegger's put down of those who attempt a philosopher's biography. "He was born, he thought, he died." Principally such a life is marked by what is undatable: the births and deaths of dynamic concepts. Yet Derrida's genial responses in the film, spiced by the occasional sharp reply (to remind his interlocutors he is not seduced, that he is a wary iconoclast) mask a deeper concern: a sense that life writing (biography) is also death writing (thanatography): "The man – to die – tomorrow," in Emily Dickinson's words.

Among the oldest definitions of philosophy is one that describes it as the study of death. Such study is intrinsic to writing in Derrida's view, writing that cannot be abstracted from thinking, and carries with it, like a mobile tabernacle, the relics – beliefs, themes, words – of philosophic ancestors. This despite the wish of every creative intelligence not to be constrained by formal philosophy, or to default into a book.

Derrida's deconstructions are anything but destructive, therefore: they insist on examining the truth or totality claim of every system, dogma, received idea; and this cannot happen without immense learning. Every monumental ideology is shown to be a constructed "universe" that revolves around a center, and that structure is carefully exposed. But how can innovative thinking, how can anything new and refreshing enter this picture, given such repetitive and depressing knowledge? This is Derrida's – and our – challenge: to accept the fact, the fate, if you wish, that the old systems, and the old words, must be deployed to create new openings rather than to undermine the adventure of thoughtfulness. Play becomes essential, then: especially the play of language, from childhood on, from babble to Babel. This plural and basically irreducible verbal energy, however, can frighten thinkers and ideologues into a "regime of phrases" (Lyotard) or impose a repressive, unjust silence.

To dramatize deconstruction via the predominantly visual medium of film would seem to be a hopeless endeavor. We can catch and condense, cinematically, the growth, opening, and fading of a flower; but can this be done with an evolving thought or linguistic process generally? Derrida, not a particularly economical thinker, writes, writes, writes, as the Wandering Jew of legend walks, walks, walks. Kirby Dick and Amy Ziering Kofman catch in their film that perpetual motion, that walking-thinking.

A disadvantage of Derrida's fluency is that its poetic quality gets lost because of the sheer mass of words. Unlike prose, language printed as poetry benefits from a lot of blank space around it. Quite unexpectedly, however, this film discovers its advantage over the medium of print: it abounds in neutral as well as interesting spaces through which the philosopher and his remarks can move. Moreover, one of the directors' many genial conceptions is to use voice-overs quoting Derrida's own texts. The poetry of his prose becomes audible as we fasten on its aphoristic quality in contrast to the surrounding visual business.

A question inevitably arises: Can film disclose a thinker's greatness, or merely his virtuosity? Here is a film worthy of its subject, yet how worthy the subject is remains partly for the future to decide. What this film confirms is that Derrida does not belong simply to those in the Parisian tumult of 1968 who were "pourfendeurs du suject," slayers of the subject.

It is true that when we say "Shakespeare" we tend to denote a corpus of plays more than a person. The author as the subjective core of a body of work is not a punctual entity, someone with fixed location. The author is "disseminated," coterminous with the work produced. Even the modernist principle of impersonality – of the "death" or "withdrawal" of the author, who gets out of the way of his own text – does not remove the impression of subjectivity.

The doctrine of impersonality, in fact, often degenerates into a quasi-classical and formalistic avoidance of heterogeneous personal features. But Derrida's interest is precisely in what is left over, left out: the "indecency" of that biographical detail, or a suppressed political aspiration, or traces of a surplus energy and desire. Heterogeneity always spoils our elegant, all-balancing equations. The stubborn remainder can be a neglected part of the body ("It is the hands and eyes that are the sites of recognition, the signs through which one identifies the Other," Derrida remarks in the film), or the timbre of a voice, or words secreted within words. "No one will ever know," Derrida writes in *Circumfession*, "what secret impels me to write...." But does he himself know that secret? The personal returns as an impenetrable zone of privacy.

Understanding this "Question of the Subject" becomes important in a society struggling to gauge the possibility of collectivism after the nightmare of totalitarian regimes. Growing up in post-war Europe this struggle was important. Derrida is far from subduing the personal in the political. His compromise is to be visibly reticent. He conspires, that is, with the affectionate and intelligent visuality of this documentary. Take his remark, partly quoted above, on the eyes: by asserting that they alone do not grow old, he emphasizes not just their physical sameness but also their listening expression, a withholding one senses in his own pursed eyes as he looks out at the camera. To look should be to retain a regard for the Other, in spite of the camera's impersonal mechanism.

Having too much peripheral vision himself, Derrida knows both the importance of focus and the inevitability of exclusions: exclusions (as Foucault also pointed out) with social and moral consequences for politics and discourse-systems. Such exclusions must be factored into one's consciousness and noted by compositional means. If Derrida, then, methodically decenters all systems, it is not in order to devalue them but rather to set in motion again, if only playfully, something too fixed or inert, so as to redeem what had been omitted or marginalized.

But there remains the moral problem of self-regard, or of the desire for self-presence. It lodges in voice as voice; and so Derrida's intellectual maneuvers, starting with *Voice and Phenomenon*, and evident in this movie about him (though always tempered by his admirable pedagogical skill and devoted attention to students), these must deliver him from a narcissism inherent in autobiography. When near the film's beginning he proposes a distinction between the "future" and "what-is-to-come" (à-venir) – a distinction important to his entire thinking, especially the postulates of indeterminacy and unpredictability – I could not resist imagining him saying: "L'avenir, c'est moi." This sentiment is literally true in the sense that despite his voluminous writings, and the attentive space this film gives him, he seems to feel at any moment his non-presence, the specter in Derrida.

Why that feeling of ghostliness, of being a phantom? He intimates a double absence: a lost center, but also the loss of the myth of the lost center. What did he actually lose? It includes a mother's love, the thousands of letters he wrote her, his native Algeria, his Jewish heritage, faith in a God to whom one might pray with genuine prayers, or confess stutteringly. All these proofs of existing, in the present, here and now, might have confirmed his identity.

But he cannot triple the center as a three-personed God, or think of Him as one whose center is everywhere and circumference nowhere. He is convinced the center cannot hold: at most it points to a displacement upwards of the need for closure, peace, rest. He rejects this repose, this quieting of the conscience. His global consciousness will not shut down. Nor is the problem solved by cultivating what he names an atheology. For when God is away the ghosts come out to play.

This caring film, however, has made Derrida more present to us, and perhaps it made a difference even to him.

In an interview with *Le Monde*, less than two months before his death, Derrida admits still being at war with himself. How many souls, positions, partial identities lived unharmonized within him? No philosopher has conveyed as forcefully, by all the literary and linguistic devices at his command, and a near-Joycean skill in mobilizing the "phonogrammatic" values of language, the discords and oppositions that cannot be mediated or dialectically stilled by a higher synthesis. Hence a style that refuses the famous French clarity. Multilingual puns, homonyms, paranomasia, neologisms and hybrid formulations, taking words apart, fusing them ("circum-fession," "nostalgérie"), pastiche, the split page, juxtapositions like that of Hegel and Genet in *Glas*, even moments that can be called Derridadaism – what literary writer is more daring?

His mistake, professionally speaking, was to be a reading philosopher, a rare species indeed. A philosopher, that is, who does not read in order to get beyond reading, to a form of propositional logic or a purged language from which all figures, ambiguities, and polysemy have been removed. The most inventive of a generation of inventive French thinkers that include Deleuze and Lyotard, he created a new form of textuality: pages haunted by what was repressed, left out, left over; pages that bring back to an oblivious present, wishfully fixated on the idea of progress, so many once living ideas, now detritus.

He does not forgo the idea of progress, however. His secret name is Eli, which stands for Elijah, forerunner of the Messiah. Yet to the very end of his life, he continued a meditation on Europe as more than a crime scene. He held that Europe since the Enlightenment rep-resented the capacity for permanent self-critique; and that the Europe of the future would strive to realize the ideal of justice inspiring the movement for human rights, and which he pursued courageously in his writings and personal interventions.

If there are complaints about his lack of parsimony in philosophic discussion or his impure style, then his project is far from being understood. The temptation he fought against, by his version of the so-called "linguistic turn," is precisely the notion of an absolutely new order of words as of politics. The quest for achieving an utopian end-state through a return to a pristine origin has always ended in a bloody purification.

Culture wars being also language wars, he wanted to leave a mark on French, basi-cally his only language. For the pressure to assimilate deprived him of both Hebrew and Arabic. French absorbed all his creative linguistic energy. A Vichy decree had made it impossible for him to remain in the Algerian public school system after 1942, so that French too was not to develop all that "naturally." Words, in any case, are never simply a medium of communication; they are fighting words, fighting not only with other words claiming to be the proper terms, but also for themselves as "mots en liberté" against dogmas mortgaging the future.

Jacques was a colleague and close friend during the eleven years he spent at Yale in the 1970s and early 1980s. His generosity, the way he gave of himself to students, and the excitement his lectures generated – intricate explications of literary and philosophical texts lasting two hours or more – made this "ghost" an unforgettable presence. His genius for friendship mitigated, no doubt, a melancholy he did not overcome. I felt a part of him lived elsewhere, and that everything he saw and read passed into and through the alembic of that region. The film described in this book makes Jacques more visible, and is invaluable in the wake of his disappearance. It comforts our sense of loss by the serious, informative, warm and accessible portrait of a brave and brilliant thinker who appeared in a needy time.

Geoffrey Hartman *YALE UNIVERSITY NEW HAVEN NOVEMBER 2004*

Blind Cinema

Nicholas Royle

IN ORDER TO SEE A PHOTOGRAPH WELL, IT IS BEST TO LOOK AWAY OR CLOSE YOUR EYES. (ROLAND BARTHES)[1]

TIME-IMAGES ARE NOT THINGS HAPPENING IN TIME, BUT NEW FORMS OF CO-EXISTENCE, ORDERING, TRANSFORMATION. (GILLES DELEUZE)[2]

WE WOULD KEEP ONLY THE WORD FILM (THE MEMBRANE, THE SENSITIVE PELLICULES, THE VEILS, THE COVERINGS, AND BY MEANS OF THIS WORD ALONE WE WOULD COVER EVERYTHING WITH A LIGHT CLOUD: I ONLY WOULD HAVE FILMED…) (JACQUES DERRIDA)[3]

How to make, and make sense of, a film about philosophy or about a philosopher talking 'on' film? How to construe film in relation to biography or story-telling? What is film anyway? And what kind of writing does it call for by way of response? I would like to explore these questions in the context of Kirby Dick and Amy Ziering Kofman's remarkable film, *Derrida*, above all by trying to attend to notions of blindness, the unseen and unforeseeable, the unshowable and the secret.

Until his death in October 2004, Jacques Derrida was often described as the world's greatest living philosopher.[4] Depending on how you choose to count the volumes and editions, and the languages in which they first appear (usually French, but sometimes English or other languages), he is the author of seventy or more books. Starting with the publication of three major works in 1967 – *Writing and Difference*, *Speech and Phenomena* and *Of Grammatology* – he produced texts at an astonishing rate.[5] He wrote on more or less everything under the sun – on philosophy, literature, science, psychoanalysis, history, religion, anthropology, politics, ethics, law, architecture, the visual arts, technology, education, aesthetics, gender, etc (and so on).[6] He even wrote an essay on 'etc (and so on)'.[7] It can indeed seem that there is little or nothing he did not write about. And every word and thing, for him, is open to question. Derrida questions *everything under the sun*. 'Everything under the sun': this phrase occurred to me out of the blue. I didn't see it coming, so to speak. There is perhaps already something of the spirit of Derrida's thinking here: he affirms chance, he stresses the fact that chance is always necessary, that experience entails the unforeseeable, that looking up at a star you fall down a well.

*

This is how Dick and Ziering Kofman's film begins. Looking over a flickering, somewhat bedazzled River Seine and Parisian landscape, mixing in with Ryuichi Sakamoto's cool, echoey, almost otherworldly music, Ziering Kofman's voice-over quotes Derrida talking about two kinds of future: the sort of future that is 'predictable' or 'foreseeable', and the sort of future that is 'totally unpredictable'. It is this second sort that he is especially interested in. Indeed the first sort is not really a future, but rather the unfolding of a program. A true future, if there is any, has to do with what we are 'completely unable to foresee'. This idea of the future is at the heart of Derrida's thinking, along with the idea of haunting and ghosts. These ideas pervade his work. As he declares at the beginning of what perhaps remains his most important and influential single book, *Of Grammatology*: 'The future can only be anticipated in the form of an absolute danger.'[8] This sense of danger, the incalculable and unforeseeable, is everywhere in his writing. And then there is the ghostly. For more than forty years Derrida explored the ways in which our lives, our perceptions, desires and memories are spooked, subject to what we cannot master or control. We are subject to effects of language, to tradition, law, and so on, in ways that are constantly slippery, troubling, strange or uncanny. What we think of as the present, today, now, for example, is never fully or purely present: it is haunted. These two Derridean ideas of the future and haunting are in fact indissociable. As he suggests at the end of *Specters of Marx* (1993): 'the thinking of the specter, contrary to what good sense leads us to believe, signals toward the future'.[9] This spectrality is at work in how he thinks about, for example, inheritance or democracy. Derrida argues that we cannot and must not take these concepts for granted. Rather he stresses that 'inheritance is never a *given*,

NOTES
1. Roland Barthes, *Camera Lucida: Reflections on Photography*, trans. Richard Howard (London: Fontana, 1984), 53.

2. Gilles Deleuze, *Negotiations*, trans. Martin Joughin (New York: Columbia University Press, 1995), 123.

3. Jacques Derrida, 'Envois', in *The Post Card: From Socrates to Freud and Beyond*, trans. Alan Bass (Chicago: Chicago University Press, 1987), 179.

4. 'Greatest living philosopher' was the phrase used by Jacqueline Rose, for example, when introducing a reading and discussion with Derrida and Hélène Cixous, at the Jewish Book Fair in London, 1 March 2004. As I hope will become evident in what follows, each word of this description would inevitably be open to question in the context of Derrida's work. He explores the idea that what we think of as 'great', in the context of a great literary or great philosophical work or a great film, might have something to do with a sense of the apparent opposite of 'great', namely with what is small, weak, humble, powerless. He is preoccupied with how 'living' or 'life' itself is caught up in death and mourning. He is interested in how philosophy is haunted by what is not philosophy, by the idea of a work of fiction, for example, or a film.

5. These works appeared in French in 1967, as *L'Écriture et la différence* (Paris: Le Seuil), *La Voix et le phénomène* (Paris: PUF), and *De la grammatologie* (Paris: Minuit). The English translations came along a little later: see *Writing and Difference*, trans. Alan Bass (London: Routledge and Kegan Paul, 1978), *Speech and Phenomena and Other Essays on Husserl's Theory of Signs*, trans. David Allison (Evanston, Illinois: Northwestern University Press, 1973), and *Of Grammatology*, trans. Gayatri Chakravorty Spivak (Baltimore: Johns Hopkins University Press, 1976).

6. For two recent books that attempt to provide some sense of the extraordinary sweep of Derrida's work, see *Jacques Derrida and the Humanities: A Critical Reader*, ed. Tom Cohen (Cambridge: Cambridge University Press, 2001) and my introductory book, *Jacques Derrida* (New York: Routledge, 2003).

7. 'Et Cetera… (and so on, und so weiter, and so forth, et ainsi de suite, und so überall, etc.)', trans. Geoffrey Bennington, in *Deconstructions: A User's Guide*, ed. Nicholas Royle (London: Palgrave, 2000), 282-305.

8. *Of Grammatology*, 5.

9. *Specters of Marx: The State of the Debt, the Work of Mourning, and the New International*, trans. Peggy Kamuf (New York: Routledge, 1994), 196, n.39.

10. *Specters of Marx*, 54.

11. *The Other Heading: Reflections on Today's Europe*, trans. Pascale-Anne Brault and Michael B. Naas (Bloomington: Indiana University Press, 1992), 98.

12. In Jacques Derrida and Bernard Stiegler, *Echographies of Television: Filmed Interviews*, trans. Jennifer Bajorek (Cambridge: Polity Press, 2002), 117.

13. For a couple of very helpful accounts of the early understanding and misunderstanding of deconstruction, see Jonathan Culler, *On Deconstruction: Theory and Criticism after Structuralism* (London: Routledge and Kegan Paul, 1983), and Martin McQuillan's *Introduction to Deconstruction: A Reader* (Edinburgh: Edinburgh University Press, 2000).

14. 'Psyche: Inventions of the Other', trans. Catherine Porter, in *Reading de Man Reading*, eds. Lindsay Waters and Wlad Godzich (Minneapolis: University of Minnesota Press, 1989), 42.

15. See 'I Have a Taste for the Secret', Jacques Derrida in conversation with Maurizio Ferraris and Giorgio Vattimo, in Derrida and Ferraris, *A Taste for the Secret*, trans. Giacomo Donis (Cambridge, England: Polity, 2001), 70.

16. 'A "Madness" Must Watch Over Thinking', trans. Peggy Kamuf, in *Points... Interviews, 1974-1994*, ed. Elisabeth Weber (Stanford: Stanford University Press, 1995), 352.

17. The first shoot was in 1995, the first screening in 2001.

18. Derrida's understanding of deferred effect (*Nachträglichkeit* in German) is crucially indebted to Freud: see, for example, 'Freud and the Scene of Writing', in *Writing and Difference*, trans. Alan Bass (London: Routledge and Kegan Paul, 1978), 196-231, esp. 203; and *Archive Fever: A Freudian Impression*, trans. Eric Prenowitz (Chicago: Chicago University Press, 1996), esp. 80.

it is always a task'.[10] And democracy is not something static and to be taken for granted either: instead, along with freedom of speech and 'freedom of the press', democracy is something that has to be affirmed, reaffirmed and even 'invented', every day.[11]

Very near the beginning of the film, Dick and Ziering Kofman present a clip from a BBC newscaster describing Jacques Derrida as 'founder of the post-structuralist mode of analysis known as deconstruction'. Deconstruction involves thinking about ghostliness, about how things are *haunted* – by difference, by otherness. As Derrida stresses: 'The spectral logic is de facto a deconstructive logic. It is in the element of haunting that deconstruction finds the place most hospitable to it.'[12] To deconstruct is to explore the effects of spectral logic. He was as aware as anyone of the tendency for 'deconstruction' to turn into a 'mere' critical method or tool: this is indeed what frequently happened in the US and Britain, in the so-called 'early days' of deconstruction, in the 1970s and 1980s. In these 'early days', deconstruction often came to be identified, in negative ways, with the sense of a program, in other words with the 'predictable' or 'foreseeable'. It was often characterised as an overly programmatic critical or theoretical discourse that sought to deconstruct, shake up or dismantle the ways in which texts and institutions are structured and understood.[13] This emphasis on deconstruction as shaking up or dismantling remains crucial, but it is important to note also that, in Derrida's own writings, deconstruction is constantly guided by a sense of the future as 'totally unpredictable'. Deconstruction entails an apprehension not only of haunting, but also of the incalculable, the unforeseeable, in other words, a certain blindness. This is what makes Derrida's work so restless, shifting, incessant: he wants to avoid words and ideas becoming (or seeming to become) static, obvious, predictable. He wants to invent. 'Deconstruction is inventive or it is nothing at all', he says.[14] He tries as far as possible to start all over again with every text he writes, in a kind of 'absolute freshness', as if he has not written anything before.[15] From one text to another, he is concerned with what he calls 'discontinuity of tone, of vocabulary, of the sentence even, and finally of address'.[16] Such forms of discontinuity are in turn provokingly figured in Dick and Ziering Kofman's film, in its often surprising switches, interruptions, cuts and shifts of focus, as it traverses back and forth, here, there, and here again, across the six years of its making, moving from France to the U.S. to South Africa and back, cut with TV images from Belgium, Britain, Poland and Australia, as well as incorporating video footage 'of its own making', and so on.[17]

There is no deconstruction without surprise. When does it happen? Integral to Derrida's thinking about the ghostly and unforeseeable is a logic of delayed effect, deferred meaning, after-effect or in French *après coup*.[18] Deconstruction involves thinking in terms of a sort of time-bomb. You never know when or how the meaning or significance of a particular image or moment in 'real life', or in a film, might emerge or change. One of the many pleasures of *Derrida* is being able to appreciate some of the intimate correspondences between Derrida's written works and his speech. Whether he is writing or speaking there is a sort of ingrained sense of engaging with the unforeseeable. As he remarks at one point in the film: 'To speak is to not see. So all speech to some extent is blind'. In this film, as in his written works, Derrida appears to be guided by Maurice Merleau-Ponty's observation: 'My own words take me by surprise and teach me what I think.'[19] At the same time, in his speech as much as in his writing, he is guided by a sense of fundamental uncertainty about who is being addressed, who is reading, listening or watching, and about *when* – about the time of reading, listening, watching. A model is thus in turn intimated for film criticism: *proceed in the dark*. Blind processing.

Deconstruction is about difference or otherness, then, and doubtless this helps to explain why it has proved such a popular term for thinking about such broad topics as race, gender, nationality and so on, as well as about literature and art. But this must not solidify into something that can be taken for granted or indeed something that you can specify in advance. Every encounter, whether with a film, a philosophical text, or whatever, is new, risky, potentially strange and surprising. Deconstruction is not only about *acknowledging* difference. It is also about being open to *being altered* in one's encounter with difference. And it is about making a difference, changing the ways we think and what we think, altering the world. Film offers a powerful way of projecting these issues. We might think of it as a singularly uncanny rendezvous of ghosts and the future. As Derrida remarks: 'the future belongs to ghosts, and modern image technology, cinema, telecommunications, etc., are only increasing the power of ghosts'.[20] On at least one occasion, indeed, he suggests that it is a film fantasy that underlies or overlays what he understands by 'deconstruction'. As he puts it in an interview in 1994, referring to the work of the French Resistance during the Second World War:

> When I was very young – and until quite recently – I used to project a film in my mind of someone who, by night, plants bombs on the railway: blowing up the enemy structure, planting the delayed-action device and then watching the explosion or at least hearing it from a distance. I see very well that this image, which translates a deep phantasmic compulsion, could be illustrated by deconstructive operations, which consist in planting discreetly, with a delayed-action mechanism, devices that all of a sudden put a transit route out of commission, making the enemy's movements more hazardous.[21]

Derrida wrote on more or less everything under the sun, I was saying. But he also wrote *on* the sun, on what is over, beyond or other than the sun. Thinking about the sun, in fact, might help to elucidate the originality of Dick and Ziering Kofman's work. Photography and film are doubtless unthinkable without light, but at the same time they necessitate a new understanding of light, of distinctions between day and night, of what might be meant by 'natural' and 'artificial' light. As Derrida remarks, in a discussion of photography and film in *Echographies of Television*: 'As soon as there is a technology of the image, visibility brings night.' When we are filmed or photographed, he says, 'we are captured by optical instruments which don't even need the light of day'. Film by its very nature entails a 'nocturnal space'.[22] At the end of 'Aphorism Countertime' (1986), an essay on Shakespeare's *Romeo and Juliet*, we encounter this strange, verbless little statement: 'A true sun, the other.'[23] This statement plays on the Prince's words at the end of Shakespeare's play: 'The sun for sorrow will not show his face.' But it might also be read as a

19. Quoted by Derrida in 'Force and Signification', in Writing and Difference, 11.

20. Quoted in Geoffrey Bennington and Jacques Derrida, Jacques Derrida, trans. Geoffrey Bennington (Chicago: Chicago University Press, 1993), 349.

21. 'I Have a Taste for the Secret', 51-2.

22. Echographies of Television, 115-7.

23. 'Aphorism Countertime', trans. Nicholas Royle, in Acts of Literature, ed. Derek Attridge (London and New York: Routledge, 1992), 433.

24. 'White Mythology: Metaphor in the Text of Philosophy', in *Margins of Philosophy*, trans. Alan Bass (Chicago: Chicago University Press, 1982), 207-71: here, 251.

25. 'Force and Signification', 27.

26. Eduardo Cadava, *Words of Light: Theses on the Photography of History* (Princeton: Princeton University Press, 1997), 5.

27. 'White Mythology', 250.

28. See 'White Mythology', 252, n.58.

29. 'White Mythology', 251.

30. In 'White Mythology', for example, Derrida discusses the way in which 'natural light' in Descartes is not itself apparently open to any doubt and thus provides the unquestioned, theological 'ether of thought'. Derrida writes: 'Natural light, and all the axioms it brings into our field of vision, is never subjected to the most radical doubt. The latter unfolds in light.... Prior to every determined presence, to every representative idea, natural light constitutes the very ether of thought and of its proper discourse. As natural, it has its source in God, in the God whose existence has been put into doubt and then demonstrated, thanks to it' (267).

31. 'Of an Apocalyptic Tone Newly Adopted in Philosophy', trans. John P. Leavey, Jr, in *Derrida and Negative Theology*, ed. Harold Coward and Toby Foshay (Albany: State University of New York Press, 1992), 51.

summation of Derrida's work. It evokes the notion of a cryptic sun, a sun that is not the sun we might suppose but a sun that is other to, other than the sun. Everything starts with the question of the sun. In 'White Mythology' (1971), perhaps his most celebrated essay on this topic, he writes: 'The very opposition of appearing and disappearing, … of day and night, of the visible and the invisible, of the present and the absent – all this is possible only under the sun.'[24] 'White Mythology' relates back in turn to one of Derrida's earliest essays, 'Force and Signification' (1963), which analyzes and questions some of the basic tenets of structuralism and thus effectively outlines an account of so-called 'poststructuralism' (years before that word is invented). In this 1963 essay he explores the idea that 'the metaphor of darkness and light (of self-revelation and self-concealment)' is 'the founding metaphor of western philosophy as metaphysics'. In this respect, he goes on to argue, 'the entire history of our philosophy is a photology, the name given to a history of, or treatise on, light'.[25] What is known as 'structuralism' is part of this history.

There is what Eduardo Cadava has called a 'secret rapport' between philosophy and photography: 'both take their life from light, from a light that coincides with the conditions of possibility for clarity, reflection, speculation, and lucidity – that is, for knowledge in general'.[26] In 'White Mythology' Derrida asks, 'What is the sun?',[27] or, in more precisely Aristotelian form: 'What is proper to the sun?' It is a question, in part, about what is going on in the crazy but at the same time seemingly logical definition of the sun that Aristotle refers to, namely 'a star appearing by day'.[28] Derrida analyzes the ways in which western philosophy has systematically associated the sun with truth, the Good, the father, and so on. He explores the ways in which the sun, from Aristotle onwards, is 'an *artificial* construction'.[29] For Derrida, *just what we do not think about,* namely the naturalness of 'natural light', is subject to radical questioning.[30] And as Dick and Ziering Kofman's film emphasises, this is a characteristic feature of deconstruction. Quite near the beginning of the film, at home in Ris-Orangis, the so-called star of the film is asked about the origin of the idea of deconstruction. Following an abrupt, ghostly cut, he says: 'I don't know who's going to be watching this.' He then seeks to stress what he calls 'the completely artificial character of this situation'. He goes on: 'One of the gestures of deconstruction is to not naturalize what isn't natural – to not assume that what is conditioned by history, institutions and society is natural.' Dick and Ziering Kofman's *Derrida* is not natural. On the contrary it affirms and exacerbates the sense that film is never natural. And Derrida himself repeatedly picks up on this, as when, for example, he is being filmed at home, wearing a nicely ironed yellow shirt, and says to the camera: 'So, this is what you call cinéma vérité?' And then he clarifies: 'I'm not really like this… I don't usually dress like this. No, …when I stay at home alone in the daytime, I don't get dressed. I stay in my pajamas and a bathrobe.'

This is not to suggest that, for Derrida, there is no difference between truth and fiction, vérité and artifice. On the contrary, his work is profoundly committed to elucidating questions of truth, reality, nature, materiality and so on. His guiding desire is for what he calls a 'new enlightenment'. His work is constantly focused on what he has called 'the enigmatic desire for vigilance, for the lucid vigil, for elucidation'.[31] And in saying this he is, as always, photosensitive, attuned to the etymological, conceptual and historical associations of these words: 'enigmatic' is related to the Greek verb *ainissesthai*, 'to speak darkly'; 'lucid' and 'elucidation' call up the Latin lux, lucis, 'light'. Derrida's focus, in other words, is also constantly deconstructive, that is to say he focuses on what is 'other' or 'enigmatic' about this desire, on how lucidity, elucidation and so many other figures apparently linking light with truth are haunted by figures of blindness. 'The other' is, after all, not only a sun, but 'a *true* sun'. Likewise his focus is on 'the true future' *(le vrai futur)* as what is completely unforeseeable. In its consistent double-focus on a new enlightenment and on blindness in philosophy, Derrida's work prompts new ways of thinking about the relationship between philosophy and film. Deconstruction calls for a thinking of blind cinema.[32]

A couple of minutes into the film we see Derrida walking in New York, accompanied by the camerawoman and others. They try to cross the road. Pointing to the camerawoman, now filming him, Derrida says: 'She sees everything around me but she is totally blind. That's the image of the philosopher who falls in the well, while looking at the star.' And then he points to himself. Derrida refers here, as he does in all of his work, to death, to blindness, for example to the danger of being run over while crossing the street while trying to film someone (the star). But in pointing to himself, he also figures himself as the philosopher tumbling in the well.[33] This brief sequence in some ways encapsulates Dick and Ziering Kofman's film. It is not certain, from one moment to the next, exactly who or what is the star, or exactly who is pointing at whom, or from what angle, watched by whom, for whom, and so on. And at the same time, all along, film-making is blind.

Derrida has not until recently been much associated with film or film studies.[34] He does of course appear elsewhere on film, on television and in films, in particular in *Ghostdance* (dir. Ken McMullen, Channel Four Films, 1984) and *D'ailleurs Derrida (Derrida's Elsewhere)* (dir. Safaa Fathy, Gloria Films, 1999). In *Ghostdance* Derrida is asked if he believes in ghosts and replies with a smile: 'That is a hard question because, you see, I am a ghost.' Here, as in Dick and Ziering Kofman's film, he draws attention to the effects of what Roland Barthes describes so powerfully in *Camera Lucida* (1980), namely 'that rather terrible thing which is there in every photograph: the return of the dead'.[35] As Derrida remarks of photography in an exchange with Bernard Stiegler: 'because we know that, once it has been taken, captured, this image will be reproducible in our absence, because we know this *already*, we are already haunted by this future, which brings our death. Our disappearance is already here… We are spectralized by the shot, captured or possessed by spectrality in advance.'[36]

Before the opening credits of Dick and Ziering Kofman's film the camera is at work in Derrida's home, in Ris-Orangis. He is looking for his keys. Already the subtlety of this film, at once playful and serious, is perhaps apparent: is this to be *cinéma à clef*? What or where are the keys to a life, to telling the story of a philosopher's life? There is the suggestion here of a filmic punning, similar to the scene a little later in which the man with the celebrated silverwhite bouffant is at the hairdresser's: through the snipping of this clip, his silverwhite hair reflected in abyssally receding mirror images, we are presented with a sort of Derridean cutting-room. In the earlier scene, on his way out, looking for his keys, he remarks in the general direction of the camera or filmmaker: 'Forgive me for not even saying hello…it's a bit difficult. So you're going to follow me?' With this question the film announces a characteristic Derridean concern. As he phrases it in *Specters of*

32. Derrida explores notions of blindness throughout his writings; but, especially in relation to drawing and the visual arts, see *Memoirs of the Blind: The Self-Portrait and Other Ruins*, trans. Pascale-Anne Brault and Michael Naas (Chicago: Chicago University Press, 1993).

33. Derrida is referring to the story of Thrales in Plato. Socrates recounts 'the story about the Thracian maidservant who exercised her wit at the expense of Thales, when he was looking up to study the stars and tumbled down a well. She scoffed at him for being so eager to know what was happening in the sky that he could not see what lay at his feet. Anyone who gives his life to philosophy is open to such mockery.' See 'Theaetetus' 174a, in *The Collected Dialogues of Plato*, ed. Edith Hamilton and Huntington Cairns (Princeton: Princeton University Press, 1961), 879.

34. For some illuminating exceptions, see Peter Brunette and David Wills, *Screen/Play: Derrida and Film Theory* (Princeton, NJ: Princeton University Press, 1989); Antony Easthope, 'Derrida and British Film Theory', in *Applying: to Derrida*, eds. John Brannigan, Ruth Robbins and Julian Wolfreys (Basingstoke and New York: Macmillan, 1996), 184-94; and Robert Smith, 'Deconstruction and Film', in *Deconstructions: A User's Guide*, ed. Nicholas Royle (Basingstoke and New York: Palgrave, 2000), 119-36. Of related interest, see also Peggy Kamuf, 'Derrida on Television', in *Applying: to Derrida*, 195-211; and Jacques Derrida and Bernard Stiegler, *Echographies of Television*.

35. Roland Barthes, *Camera Lucida*, 9.

36. *Echographies of Television*, 117.

37. *Specters of Marx*, 10.

38. 'I have never known how to tell a story' is how his book *Mémoires* begins: see *Mémoires: for Paul de Man*, trans. Cecile Lindsay, Jonathan Culler and Eduardo Cadava (New York: Columbia University Press, 1986), 3.

39. 'The Madness of the Day', in *The Station Hill Blanchot Reader: Fiction and Literary Essays*, trans. Lydia Davis, Paul Auster and Robert Lamberton, ed. George Quasha (Barrytown, New York: Station Hill Press, 1999), 191-9. Derrida discusses this brief text at length in 'Living On/ Border Lines', trans. James Hulbert, in Harold Bloom et al., *Deconstruction and Criticism* (New York: Seabury Press, 1979), 75-176; 'Title (to be specified)', trans. Tom Conley, *SubStance*, 31 (1981): 5-22; and 'The Law of Genre', trans. Avital Ronell, in *Acts of Literature*, ed. Derek Attridge (London and New York: Routledge, 1992), 221-52.

40. 'The Madness of the Day', 199.

41. 'The Madness of the Day', 195.

Marx: 'What does it mean to follow a ghost? And what if this came down to being followed by it, always, persecuted perhaps by the very chase we are leading?'[37] If Dick and Ziering Kofman follow Derrida, Derrida is also following them. *Derrida* is a film about following (going after, attending, keeping one's eye on, believing, grasping or understanding), about the compulsiveness *and* ghostliness of following, of following the camera, of following the story, of following a film.

But *Derrida* is also about the impossibility of following, about the consequences and effects of Derrida's work vis-à-vis the 'story of a life', about the idea that Derrida cannot tell a story. 'I've always said I can't tell a story', he tells Ziering Kofman in the film, in the context of her asking him about the idea of biography and anecdote.[38] He says that he always feels that 'the telling is somehow inadequate to the story I'd want to tell'. He is referring back to one of the funniest moments in the film, in which he and his wife Marguerite are asked: 'How did you two meet?' Ziering Kofman asks Marguerite, 'Do you remember the first time you saw Jacques?' and Marguerite is starting to recall ('Yes, yes. In the snow') when Jacques interrupts, gently mocking the questioner: 'She seems to be surprised that we actually remember.' But where does this scene begin, and who interrupts first? There is the dinner party at the home of René and Chantal Major. Amy Ziering Kofman says, obviously not for the first time: 'How did you two meet? Wait a second – cut.' Then Derrida remonstrates: 'How can I start to think about responding to your question when you interrupt me to adjust the lights and then you interrupt me a second time – I can't do it.' Dick and Ziering Kofman play with the desire for biographical information ('raw facts' as Derrida calls them in this scene), the desire for anecdote and revelation. And so does Derrida. It becomes difficult to tell who is telling this story about the inability to tell a story. Except that, in a sense, it is the story of film itself, this film and film as such. It is as if Derrida's proclaimed inability or refusal to tell a story were 'made for film', as if film were an uncannily appropriate 'place' for this impossible story. When watching and hearing the repeated question 'How did you two meet?', it is difficult not to think of Maurice Blanchot's extraordinary short story or récit ('narrative' or 'account') 'The Madness of the Day', about which Derrida wrote in detail on a number of occasions.[39] The narrator of 'The Madness of the Day' is met with a demand from certain 'authorities': 'Tell us "*just* exactly" what happened.' Unable to comply, the narrator says: 'I had to acknowledge that I was not capable of forming a story out of these events... But this explanation only made them more insistent.' 'How did you two meet?' Cut. 'How did you two meet?'

Blanchot's 'The Madness of the Day' concludes with the memorable line: 'A story? No. No stories, never again.'[40] Dick and Ziering Kofman's *Derrida* offers a filmic enactment of this conclusion: the 'How did you two meet?' is repeated, replayed, disseminated, put into an abyss (*mise en abyme*) as a sort of *Groundhog Day* scenario in which we see Derrida (now in Los Angeles) watching this scene on a TV screen and, again asked about it (now in Laguna), saying: 'I was moved by the scene, I liked it a lot. But I liked it precisely because we don't say anything'. Blanchot's text is not a film, and yet it perhaps allows us to see how *Derrida* works its own singular 'madness of the day' *as a film*. Blanchot's first person narrator (relating his bizarre, undecidably 'autobiographical', 'fantastical' and 'surreal' account) tells us: 'In the end, I grew convinced that I was face to face with the madness of the day. That was the truth: the light was going mad, the brightness had lost all reason.'[41] Derrida's work in turn seeks to attend to its own madness of the day, a photological madness. As he suggests in an interview, one has to proceed 'at every moment… without assurance': 'madness, a certain "madness" *must* keep a lookout over every step, and finally watch over thinking, as reason does also'.[42] Playing with the light, with the ghostly, nocturnal and artificial (*Derrida* was finally rendered, color corrected and matched as '4 p.m. light'[43]), trying to reckon with the subject of Derrida, his madness, in its own way (as Derrida stresses in the film, this is Dick and Ziering Kofman's autobiography as much as Derrida's filmic biography), *Derrida* highlights the desire for a story and for revelation (more light!), but organizes itself through a Blanchotic insistence on 'no stories', an affirmation of the inadequacy or impossibility of any single *récit*, a breaking up of the linearity of narrative, an assertion and enactment of deferred sense, an ironic, funny, cutting emphasis on the necessarily disruptive and unforeseeable effects of interruption. What kind of film is Dick and Ziering Kofman's *Derrida*? Bio-pic? Autobio-pic? Reflexive documentary? Philosophical film-study? In its singular and ironic fashion, Dick and Ziering Kofman's work throws a new light on film and philosophy, on documentary and biography, the blinding light of something like a madness of the filmic day, a sense of that 'demented sun' of which Derrida speaks in his work on Blanchot.[44]

To improvise (literally, to deal with what is not foreseen, *improvisus* in Latin) is perhaps impossible, or at any rate, as the voice-over in the film recalls from an unpublished interview from 1982: 'I believe in improvisation and I fight for improvisation. But always with the belief that it's impossible. And there where there is improvisation I am not able to see myself. I am blind to myself.' 'It's uncanny, bizarre', Derrida remarks at one point in the film, when asked about a portrait of himself at an exhibition at the Cathedral Gallery in Paris. Initially he says that the exhibit makes him 'very anxious', but then he affirms: *J'accepte*. This 'I accept', 'I agree to it, yes', recalls his play on this phrase in the 'Envois' in *The Post Card* (1980): 'j'accepte', yes, I accept, in this little verbal dissolve of 'Jacques' and 'I accept'.[45] In this encounter with a portrait of himself, in the strange filmic portrait entitled *Derrida*, Derrida affirms, uneasily, the need to accept strangeness, to affirm what is different from oneself, but also to affirm oneself as different, at odds with oneself. 'J'accepte' is a signature-effect (me, yes, Jacques, it's Jacques here) that testifies to the double bind of narcissism: the more of it, the less of it. Inscribing the proper name is a way of losing it. Anyone can say 'j'accepte'. Ziering Kofman's voice-over comes in at this point, aptly recalling an interview in *Points* concerned with what Derrida calls 'a new narcissism that is much more open to the movement of the other as other'. As he notes in the film, in the context of some reflections on Narcissus: 'To see oneself [as Narcissus does] is a form of blindness'.

Dick and Ziering Kofman's film emphasises the visual and ocular, the specular associations of narcissism and spectrality, but it also makes us think about touch and tangibility, about the figure of the hand and hands. 'I'm very interested in the hands of philosophers,' Derrida tells us: '… the hand changes [over the years]… but the hands and the eyes are the site of recognition… They are also the parts of the body we see least easily. It's difficult to have an image of our own act of looking or to have a true image of our hands as they are moving. It's the Other who knows what our eyes and hands are like.' There are numerous moments in the film where we are made especially aware of Derrida's hands, on

41. 'The Madness of the Day', 195.

42. 'A "Madness" Must Watch Over Thinking', trans. Peggy Kamuf, in Points… Interviews, 1974-1994, ed. Elisabeth Weber (Stanford: Stanford University Press, 1995), 363.

43. My thanks to Kirby Dick and Amy Ziering Kofman for this information.

44. See 'The Law of Genre', 252.

45. See 'Envois', in The Post Card, 26, 34, and passim.

46. *Specters of Marx*, 7.

47. *Roland Barthes, Camera Lucida, 80-1 (trans. modified).*

48. *Echographies of Television*, 115.

49. *Gilles Deleuze, Cinema 2: The Time-Image, trans. Hugh Tomlinson and Robert Galeta (London: Athlone Press, 1989), 204-5.*

50. *Cinema 2: The Time-Image*, 205.

the move, crucially involved in what he is saying. We watch him putting lids on pens, filling his pipe, picturing the size of one of the stones discovered in his mother's kidney, shaping the dark urn-like objects in the Derrida Archive at Irvine. At one especially memorable moment the sound of his voice is removed altogether and we are left watching these remarkable gesticulating hands. We don't hear any longer what he is saying, as his body fades into other images, the silhouette of someone walking across the screen, an image of Derrida with a book, one Derrida giving way to another. If Shakespeare's *Hamlet* haunts Dick and Ziering Kofman's film, this would consist not only in what Derrida calls (in the context of a reading of the play) 'the *visor effect*', namely the sense that 'we do not see who looks at us', but also in the motions of the hand.[46] As with the appearance of the Ghost in Shakespeare's play, Derrida's opening question, 'So you're going to follow me?', entails a certain beckoning – like the Ghost 'wav[ing]' the spectator towards 'a more removèd ground' (I, iv, 42) – in the silent language of hands. In *Camera Lucida* Barthes writes: 'From a real body, which was there, proceed radiations that come to touch me, I who am here… The photograph [or film] of the missing being … comes to touch me like the delayed rays of a star'.[47] What does it mean to be touched by a film, as if by delayed effect, by 'the delayed rays of a star'? Referring to Barthes's words, in one of his interviews with Stiegler, Derrida comments: 'When Barthes grants such importance to touch in the photographic experience, it is insofar as the very thing one is deprived of, as much in spectrality as in the gaze which looks at images or watches film and television, is indeed tactile sensitivity. The desire to touch, the tactile effect or affect, is violently summoned by its very frustration, summoned to come back, like a ghost, in the places haunted by its absence… The specter… is not tangible.'[48]

Dick and Ziering Kofman's *Derrida* is a meddling work. It interferes with the 'life' and 'nature' of film, through what Derrida says, through the medley of quotations, voice-overs and 'in-person' interviews, as well as through his expressions and gestures, and through the often unexpected angles and perspectives in which we are presented with these. Derrida knows, and the film knows, that his hands are spectrally signalling (towards) the untouchable. It is as if we were watching a strange and singular adventure film, seeking new and different ways of thinking and experiencing film.

Trying to come up with another way of describing what sort of film Dick and Ziering Kofman have made, we might think of Gilles Deleuze's phrase, 'a cinema of the brain'. '"Give me a brain"', Deleuze argues, constitutes one of the most significant figures of modern cinema: it is a matter of 'a cinema of the brain, which reveals the creativity of the world, its colors aroused by a new space-time, its powers multiplied by artificial brains.'[49] Stanley Kubrick is, for Deleuze, perhaps the most powerful example, because in his films 'the world itself is a brain, there is identity of brain and world, as in the great circular and luminous table in *Doctor Strangelove*, the giant computer in *2001 A Space Odyssey*, the Overlook hotel in *The Shining*.'[50] Dick and Ziering Kofman's film is, after all, explicitly and emphatically about a 'great thinker'. The principal publicity blurb for *Derrida* runs: 'What if someone came along who CHANGED not the way you THINK about everything but EVERYTHING about the way you think?' We are constantly being directed, prompted, invited into thinking about Derrida's brain. As his brother René says in the film: 'we ask ourselves, "How does he do it?" How must his mind work to be able to come up with all these philosophical thoughts? Because we have brains as well, and we cannot come up with such things. Why him?' If *Derrida* is about some new species of 'cinema of the brain', however, it is very much a spectral brain that is at issue. That is in part what is suggested by the voice-overs that punctuate the film: at moments they can seem to resonate as eerie disembodiments, as if we were inside this thinker's mind or as if there were no longer any inside. *Donovan's Brain* meets *Being John Malkovich*. The pleasure of being able to think that we can see Derrida thinking, in the course of this film, mingles with the pleasure of knowing that we cannot. Blindness is the law. The female voice-over, underscored by the echoey accompaniment of Sakamoto's music, also figures as a sort of Echo to Derrida's Narcissus. One becomes the other, as we find when we see Derrida (or Derrida's reflection in a mirror) talking about this in the film, 'acting as both Narcissus and Echo, at one and the same time'. But as he also makes clear, Echo and Narcissus finally call to be thought of as 'two blind people'. There are so many echoes, reflectors and reflections composing this film. Overall, we are left with a curiously disorienting sense of surface and superficiality, as if with a film over our eyes, the world of Derrida's filmed body, his eyes, hands, mouth and voice. It is as if there were a film over the film, a film over film, a peculiar caul or light cloud, something at once newly visible and newly blinding.[51]

One of the striking characteristics of a 'cinema of the brain', in Deleuze's account, is the prominence of what he calls the time-image. The time-image is not an image *of* something: rather, it is what is produced through the effects of 'false continuity and irrational cuts'.[52] As he puts it in an interview: 'Time-images are nothing to do with before and after, with succession. Succession was there from the start as the law of narration. Time-images are not things happening in time, but new forms of co-existence, ordering, transformation.'[53] We have already remarked on some of the ways in which Dick and Ziering Kofman's film stresses a logic of blindness in any and every point of view, illustrates a ghostliness of time, disturbs and dislocates the desire for narrative. Estranging any 'naturalness' of light or image, insistently affirming discontinuity and interruption, it tampers with notions of succession or 'following'. The logic of the time-image can show up in a certain disjunction or dissociation of seeing and hearing. An example would be when we witness the removal of the sound of Derrida's voice while still faced with the moving language of his hands. Another example is when students meet Derrida at Northwestern University. One of the students says: 'Listening to you speak just elucidated your texts just so much for me.' She is announcing a truth that the film more generally bears out: it is extremely instructive to *hear* Derrida. Another student says: 'I read one of your novels over the summer… I just wanted to hear you speak so I could understand it better.' This is a funny compliment of course, since Derrida has never published a novel. But who is this man now standing beside him fiddling with the microphone on Derrida's lapel? A third student is saying to Derrida: 'I started reading about negative theology and I was wondering if there was any connection…' At this point we have what the transcript calls 'microphone interference': the man is adjusting the microphone, and we can no longer make out what Derrida is saying. We don't know whether to see or hear a connection in this disconnection, between the question of negative theology and his effective cutting off of Derrida. Still this disconnection of sound and image,

51. In this context it is perhaps not without interest that, in the same passage of 'Envois' in which he speaks of the 'light cloud' (see epigraph and note 3 above), Derrida characterizes the Envois as a 'small private cinema' (The Post Card, 179).

52. Cinema 2: The Time-Image, ix.

53. Gilles Deleuze, Negotiations, 123.

54. 'Envois', in The Post Card, 3-256. Cf. also, for example, Prégnances (Paris: Brandes, 1993); Right of Inspection, trans. David Wills, with photographs by Marie-Françoise Plissart (New York: Monacelli Press, 1998); 'Telepathy', trans. Nicholas Royle, in Martin McQuillan, ed., Deconstruction: A Reader (Edinburgh: Edinburgh University Press, 2000), 496-526; and 'Ants', trans. Eric Prenowitz, in Oxford Literary Review, vol.24 (2002), 17-42.

55. 'Passions: "An Oblique Offering" ', trans. David Wood, in On the Name, ed. Thomas Dutoit (Stanford: Stanford University Press, 1995), 26.

56. On the eye-line, see Echographies of Television, 115.

57. Specters of Marx, 101.

58. Echographies of Television, 120.

59. See 'The Time is Out of Joint', trans. Peggy Kamuf, in Deconstruction is/in America: A New Sense of the Political, ed. Anselm Haverkamp (New York: New York University Press, 1995), 14-38. The question 'So long?' is taken from Hamlet, III, ii, 127.

60. Archive Fever, 100-1.

on the subject of the relation between deconstruction and negative theology, seems eerily 'fitting'.

Finally, *Derrida* only shows what it shows. Derrida talks teasingly, towards the end, about the sex lives of philosophers, about the idea of watching a documentary about Hegel or Heidegger and being able to hear them speak about 'their sex lives': 'I want them to speak about the part that love plays in their lives. So you could take a microphone up to Hegel...' The 'sexual life' of these philosophers is not something they talk about. Derrida then suggests that his work is different, and this is in many respects true: several of his texts are profoundly and explicitly concerned with 'sexual life'. The 'Envois' section of *The Post Card* (1980) is, I would suggest, one of the most erotic texts in western literature.[54] But at the same time of course Derrida does not tell us about his own sex life. We are left with a sense of someone (Jacques Derrida) and something (the film) determinedly playful, resistant, cryptic. Derrida only says what he says, just as Blanchot's narrator does in *The Madness of the Day*. And *Derrida* only shows what it shows. In this way it presents us with a sense of the secret, as Derrida formulates it in an essay entitled 'Passions': *'There is something secret. But it does not conceal itself.'*[55] The film ends with the camera and us watching Derrida watching. It is not clear who or what he is watching. The eye-line (or what he elsewhere glosses as 'the fact of looking eye to eye') is missing.[56] In these closing moments, we are perhaps more than ever aware of the peculiarity of the screen, its ghostliness. As he remarks in *Specters of Marx:* 'a screen always has, at bottom, in the bottom or the background that it is, a structure of disappearing apparition.'[57] Here at the close of the film, just before it disappears, it is difficult not to recall also his comments on the actress Pascale Ogier who appeared in *Ghostdance* and died shortly after its release: 'I am dead, I know what I'm talking about from where I am, and I'm watching....'[58] There is something especially strange and painful about the silent vigilance of this ending in which the camera lingers on the face of the star so long. 'So long?' This is the question Hamlet asks, incredulously, in response to Ophelia's telling him how long it is since his father died; but it also serves as the enigmatic epigraph to Derrida's essay on Shakespeare's play, an essay that specifically identifies mourning with the sense that 'the time is out of joint'.[59] The epigraph is enigmatic in part because it carries a suggestion of the contemporary English idiom for saying goodbye. 'So long?' Derrida watches in silence. How long will this image last? How long will the film endure? For how long, and how, will it be remembered? This steady but restless final image of Derrida's and the camera's vigilance is accompanied by the disembodied voice-over reciting words from *Archive Fever* (1993). These are words about Freud but also inevitably about Derrida (he who, as we have just been told, has never been and would never consider being 'in psychoanalysis', but who nevertheless has also just admitted to the existence of 'traumatic breaks' in his life). They concern the question of 'the inviolable secret': 'We will always wonder what he may have kept of his unconditional right to secrecy... What was concealed? What did he conceal even beyond the intention to conceal, to lie, or to perjure?'[60] In the end, in a movement at once cryptic and graceful, Derrida turns his face away, off, elsewhere.

*

Backtrack by way of postscript or epilogue. Let us pause on a scene from somewhere near the middle, flashing back, wrapping up or unwrapping another thought of this film, a scene that seems especially simple but haunting. It is called 'Radio/Eggplant (Kitchen, Ris-Orangis)': 'Derrida prepares lunch for himself while listening to news on the radio.' The radio announces (in the English translation given in the subtitles): 'The military chief of the Hezbollah, the pro-Iranian movement, was killed this morning in South Lebanon by an attack from an Israeli helicopter which destroyed the car of the Hezbollah chief. Israel then launched an operation targeting many positions of the Hezbollah in South Lebanon. In Rwanda, the refugees are continuing their exodus. There are now 45,000 who are walking towards Tanzania.' In her essay, 'Making Derrida – An Impression', Amy Ziering Kofman expresses regret that the film had not 'spelled out less obliquely the political import of [Derrida's work]'. As the film itself suggests, however, what is most powerful can also be oblique.[61] The more or less chance juxtaposition or synchronicity of the news from the Middle East and Africa with Derrida preparing his lunch perhaps has as much to say about the 'political import' of his work as the filmed visit to Nelson Mandela's prison-cell on Robben Island or the clip from the post-lecture discussion on forgiveness at the University of Western Cape, in South Africa, in 1998. In this juxtaposition or synchronicity there is a disjunction or dissociation of another sort. It is tempting to say that the appeal of this scene lies, at least in part, in the fact that Derrida doesn't say anything. We hear the radio with him, and in a strange sense can perhaps share that hearing. Yet there is at the same time also a remarkable sense of solitude in this scene. As he says in and of his autobiographical text entitled 'Circumfession': 'It only happens to me.'[62] From so many texts, essays and interviews, we can gather a great deal about what Derrida thinks about 'the world war' that is centered on the 'appropriation of Jerusalem', about genocide and terrorism, ethnic cleansing and the 'hatred' sowed by 'nationalisms of native soil'.[63] Derrida does not eat. Or rather, we do not see him eat. It is another instance of what is unseen, unshown, a filmic blindspot or blindfold. We watch Derrida take the eggplant out of the fridge and set it on the table. The food is wrapped in clingfilm. After helping himself to a couple of slices, he replaces the clingfilm. Once more, this image that clings, so long, image of a film in and on film. And, in a peculiarly poignant irony, he is of course touching it, fingering the film. Then he turns on the radio. Biodegradable or not, film is something, as he has telegrammatically noted elsewhere, 'to be processed'.[64]

61. The 'oblique' has a complex place in the context of Derrida's work: for a discussion of this, see 'Passions: "An Oblique Offering" ', esp. 12-14.

62. 'Circumfession', in Jacques Derrida, trans. Geoffrey Bennington (Chicago: Chicago University Press, 1993), 305. Cf. 'Envois', in The Post Card, 135.

63. To name just a small number of obvious texts in this context, see Specters of Marx; The Gift of Death, trans. David Wills (Chicago: Chicago University Press, 1995); Negotiations: Interventions and Interviews, 1971-2001, ed. Elizabeth Rottenberg (Stanford: Stanford University Press, 2002); and Philosophy in a Time of Terror: Dialogues with Jürgen Habermas and Jacques Derrida (Chicago: Chicago University Press, 2003).

64. 'Living On / Border Lines', 77-8.

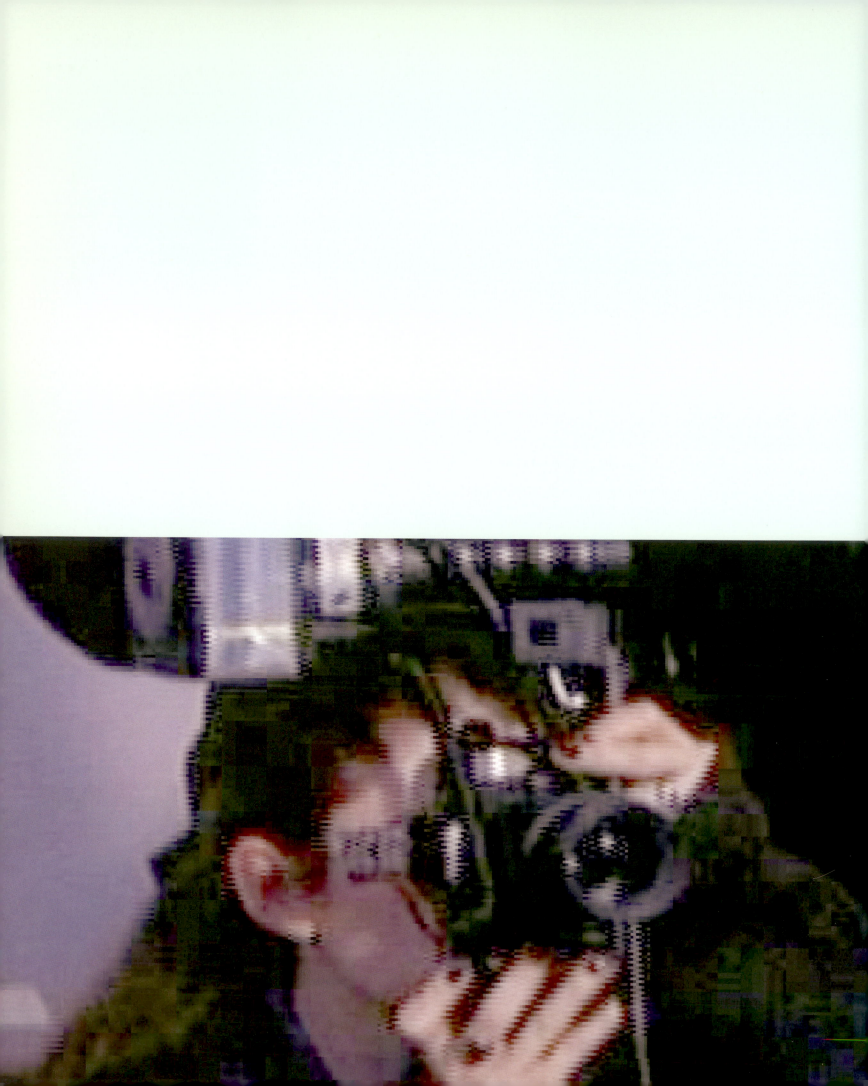

Amy Ziering Kofman

MAKING 'DERRIDA' – AN IMPRESSION

or:

HOW TO MAKE A FILM ABOUT SOMEONE WHO DOESN'T WANT A FILM MADE ABOUT THEM AND WHOSE WORK – TO PUT IT MILDLY – AT FIRST GLANCE WOULD APPEAR TO RESIST ANY AND ALL CINEMATIC TREATMENT

The idea to make a film 'on' Jacques Derrida occurred to me while I was watching him deliver a lecture to students at a UC campus in the early nineties. As I sat in the audience listening to him speak, I remember thinking that – given his powerful brilliance, prominent stature and the unique global influence of his work since the mid 1960's – some type of cinematic record should be made of him, at the very least, for archival and historical purposes. With these thoughts in mind, I approached him after the lecture, reintroduced myself (I'd been a student of his in graduate school at Yale in the early eighties), and asked if he'd agree to participate in a documentary film project.[1]

After some parrying,[2] Derrida gave his consent and that is pretty much how the film got underway. At that time I wasn't sure what type of film I was going to make, but I was sure that I wanted to do something that would in no way dumb down or betray the sophistication and complexity of his work, but would rather, in its own way, testify to its formidable power and import. In short, the ambition for the film was always quite high even though, at the time of conception, I had very little idea how I would ever arrive at translating that ambition cinematically.

From the project's outset, I was, though, quite clear about what I did not want the film to be. I knew that I did not want it to be a conventional PBS or BBC type documentary narrative that biographically recounted facts about Derrida's life in a standard documentary fashion. My inter-

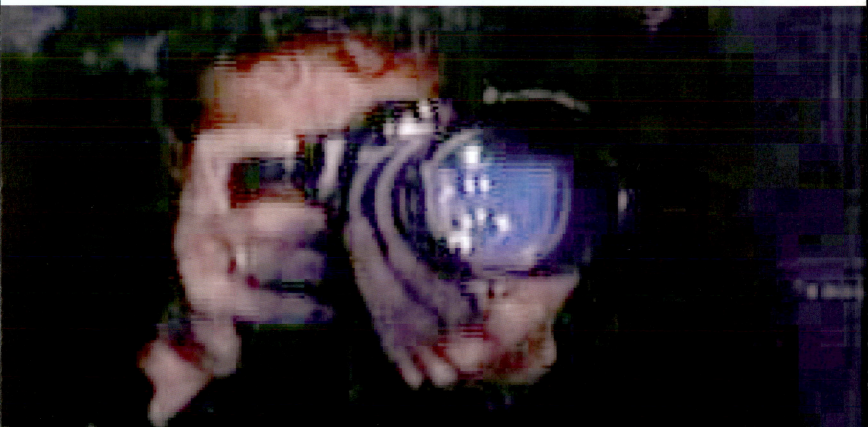

est was primarily in Derrida's work, and, as such, I was not interested in producing something along the conventional narrative lines meted by the standard grammar of Western documentaries; a narrative grammar whose ideological implications Derrida's writing had, if nothing else, effectively taken to task for the past some four plus decades.

I met Kirby Dick in 1996 when my friend, Hollywood film editor Debbie Zeitman, invited me to go with her to see a rough cut of a documentary being edited by a friend of hers, Dody Dorn, in Silverlake.[3] The film was Kirby's *Sick,* and I was so taken with it that I stayed afterwards to talk with Kirby about it, as well as see if he had any advice or ideas to offer to me concerning my work on Derrida. By this time I had already completed two major shoots with Derrida and was about to embark on a third. To make a long story short, more conversations ensued, and within a year's time Kirby and I had decided to work together as co-directors on the film. We felt that Kirby's experience in documentary film production as well as his interest in French psychoanalytic theory, coupled with my familiarity with Derrida's written work could somehow combine to make the film we both agreed the subject demanded.

Hollywood producer Robert Evans once said something like: "any film that is made without considerable strife will have highly underwhelming results." To this day, many of my friends and family believe that the real award winning film would have been the "Making of Derrida". Kirby and I had both an extremely productive and heated partnership – we are both opinionated and strong willed and that, to put it mildly, makes for rather interesting collaborative situations. Our deal with one another was that everything had to be mutually agreed upon and signed off on or it didn't end up in the film; and so edits would remain in the cut as long as either of us wanted them to, until some mutual agreement was reached. This was a fruitful and exhausting arrangement and, consequently, differences of opinion often didn't resolve in the most genteel or timely fashion.

While Kirby and I disagreed about many things over the course of the next five years, we never disagreed about the central ambition for the film we hoped to make – that is, the initial two precepts that had impelled me to embark on this project were never a contested issue between us, but rather an unequivocally agreed upon motivating assumption: first, that the film should attempt to honor and not betray the integrity of Derrida's critical work, and second, that the film should also, in its own way, bear witness to his works' significance and power.

Derrida and I had our share of difficulties as well. Even in the best possible situations, documentary subjects almost always have a complicated relationship with their filmmakers, and Jacques was no different from the norm in this regard. Granted he perhaps had even better reasons

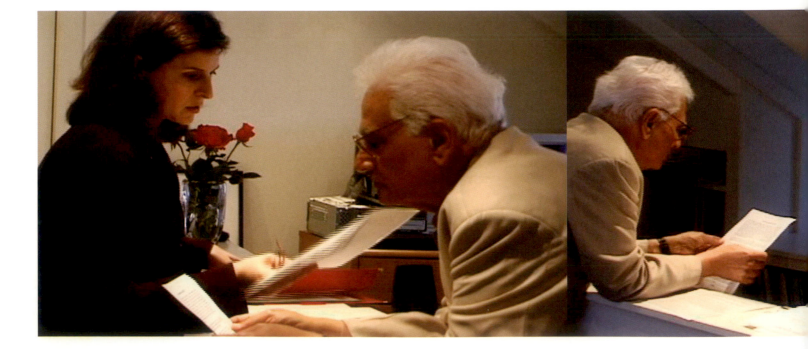

than others to act on his distrust: As a world renowned figure and global celebrity in his own right, he had extensive firsthand knowledge of the exploits of the media, and thus harbored a very keen and justified intellectual suspicion of all media enterprises. When one considers as well that words are pretty much the exclusive currency of his trade, it's easy to understand his vigilance and perception that the stakes for him in making this film were extremely high.

In fact, the deal we had with Jacques was that before the film could ever be released publicly, he would have the right to view it and exercise any type of final cut. That is, anything he wanted removed would be removed or the film would not go out. No questions asked. When he did see the final cut of the film (a cut that approximated what we were preparing to submit for entry to Sundance) he initially said to me: "It's ok. It can go out." He then called me the next day with what I remember he qualified as: "A request and a favor." The "request" was that we remove a scene which showed Jacques and me discussing the terms of our filmmaking contract. The "favor" was that we remove a scene in which we showed Jacques in an over the shoulder shot eating yogurt in his kitchen.

It's important to make clear that other than agreeing to the times and places we were allowed to shoot him (which are, though, rather significant directorial decisions in an unscripted documentary) Jacques had absolutely no input over the content and nature of the actual film. It was for that reason that he wanted us to remove the contract scene for he felt, somewhat rightly, that it could be misconstrued as indicating that he had had more collaborative input on the film than he did. Although we didn't exactly agree that this scene would necessarily read to audiences in the way he envisioned, we did understand his perspective on this matter and thought this request was fair. And although we liked the yogurt scene, its ultimate inclusion was of no significant import to us. We understood that its removal was requested because the scene just made him viscerally uncomfortable, and his request to omit it was made essentially the same way one decides whether or not to include certain photos in a photo album. For Jacques the excision of the yogurt scene wasn't really a big deal (hence the qualification of the request for it's removal as 'a favor') and as we likewise had no great investment in it, we promptly removed it.

Our film had no real structural model or precedent. Works I referred to or watched in preparation for editing were: Wim Wenders' *Notebooks and Cities*, Chris Markers' *Sans Soleil*, parts of Robert Altman's *The Player*, and Stephen Soderbergh's *The Limey*. I also watched quite a bit of Godard – *Two or Three Things I Know About Her, La Chinoise, JLG by JLG* as well as some documentaries he had made for French television. Also, in preparation I read and reread most of Derrida's oeuvre. This whole process took about

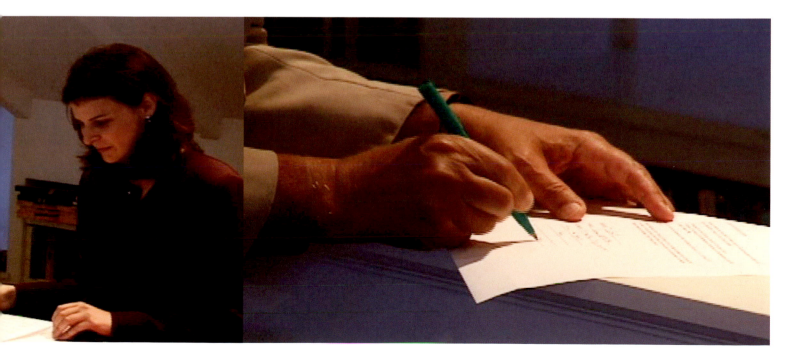

seven to nine months. I approached the works chronologically, starting with the early works and moving forward. Again, I wasn't sure what this would all add up to, but felt it was something that needed to be done.

We decided the best way to determine the structure of the film was to begin working with the material. Due to logistics and each of our needs to juggle our work on this film with our work on other projects, we felt that the way that made the most sense was for us each to work independently cutting footage and then get together to watch and discuss our results. Kirby can operate editing equipment and is an excellent and experienced film editor. Up until this time I, though, had had very little hands on editing experience, so whereas Kirby predominantly worked alone on his editorial efforts, I used an editor or assistant editor to work with me on mine. Our attempts greatly varied in tone and style, with much of the work produced at that time falling more in line with the type of editing that would occur in an experimental or art film if one were to attempt to qualify it.[4]

Working with Matt Clarke, I decided to break up the material by thematic topic (biography, death, archive, etc.) and use placards with phonetic spellings to introduce each section. (eg.: bī-'ä-gr&-fē for biography, etc.). Early on, my husband, Gil Kofman, had also, independently done a great deal editorial work on the film, extensively playing with the material in novel ways. All of my solo editing sessions benefited greatly from Gil's work and I incorporated a great deal of his material in my sequences and assemblies. In fact one of his initial editorial conceits, though greatly refined and reworked by Kirby, appears in the film's final incarnation: the mis-en-abyme sequence in which Marguerite and Jacques, while perched on a couch at the Major's house, discuss how they first met. Several of Gil's additional cuts, although they didn't make it into the finished film, appear in the deleted scenes section of our DVD.

Somewhere in the middle of this editing process, I came up with the idea of thinking about the structure of the film in terms of a musical metaphor. Since our film had no storyline or dramatic narrative per se, I thought it might be of help to think about structuring it the way a fugue is structured – that is, with themes that are introduced and repeated, but, in their repetition, augment, weave, complicate and compete with one another – producing a steady and ever more rich and complex build that would not necessarily resolve in some neat and unifying fashion. With this metaphor in mind, the film began to fall more quickly into place. Working with Kathryn Himoff (one of the many editors who worked for a brief time on the film), the three of us labored to piece together scenes that had already been cut, and to layer the themes we'd decided would be explored in our film: biography, archive, love, genealogy, anecdote, the signature/countersignature, filmmaking, etc. As all of these themes are to a degree inter-implicated, it wasn't especially difficult to piece them together in the fugue-like manner we were attempting to forge.

As editing continued, we became more and more certain that we wanted the film to reflect, both thematically and structurally, some of the fundamental precepts that shape and inform many of Derrida's written works. That is, taking the lead from the way in which Derrida structures his own arguments, we wanted the film to cinematically mime or rehearse certain elements explored in his work. For example, Derrida's written arguments are not presented in a linear straightforward manner, but rather, are always juggling various elements at one and the same time. This is not an arbitrary or aesthetic stylistic gesture on Derrida's part (although it has often been misread as such), but rather is a calculated strategy invoked to further demonstrate and support arguments being "thematically" made, as well as to continually make the point, in its own right, about the various levels always linguistically at play in any argument and the profound political and ideological stakes of that play. That is to say that if Derrida's written works are always to some degree intent on addressing an inveterate and intractable polysemy 'always already' at work in language, Derrida himself enlists this very polysemy quite purposively in his writing to further demonstrate his theoretical contentions.

Taking our cue from this Derridean strategy, we, likewise aspired to edit the film's footage so that it would operate on several levels at the same time. To give just one example, the opening quote concerning 'l'avenir' and 'the future' was selected to not only present Derrida's thematic thinking about l'avenir and the future, but also to concomitantly act as an allegory for our own act of filmmaking – with l'avenir figuring (albeit a bit reductively) for the element of unpredictability endemic to any documentary film project; (i.e.: You may agree to a rendezvous with a film crew at a future date but there is nothing predictable about what will transpire and be recorded at that time.) This implied allegory extends (again somewhat crudely) as well to the position of the viewer watching the film. (i.e.: You may know what you are engaging in when you purchase your ticket, but your response to and interaction with the material on the screen is more in the spirit of what Derrida describes as 'l'avenir' than what he refers to as 'the future.')

Similarly, our cuts were selected with an eye toward structural complication to rehearse and further certain theoretical concerns. And so a verité shot of Derrida making an off hand remark in jest about his own narcissism cuts to a voice reciting one of his more complex theoretical formulations about narcissism. Each scene now reading differently as a result of the juxtaposition – the casual remark gaining a completely different valence and weight, and our over-

arching thematic about the complex nexus between one's life and work subtly expounded by this editorial choice. Similarly, Derrida's impromptu discourse on the eyes and the hands ends with a cut from Derrida's expostulating face to a static shot of a painted portrait of his visage hanging in a gallery; the impenetrable gaze now reading differently given the preceding ocular oratory, and a cut which at first might have read as an incidental or textbook graphic match cut (based on relationships of contingency or accident) now points as well, more directly, to issues of spectatorship and specularity.

As yet another example of how we chose to deploy editing to raise theoretical issues, Derrida's admonition to the Australian news journalist in response to her question regarding the Seinfeld sitcom to "turn off the TV and read" is immediately followed by a shot of Derrida himself somewhat aimlessly changing channels at home. This cinematic montage rehearses a certain destabilization of the intractable authority of a univocal authorial perspective (i.e., that one should really turn off the t.v.); and this destabilization echoes a turn similar to that invoked internally in the scene of the burning crib joke revelation, a scene in which the disparity between a subject's articulation – "Between my sister and myself there was always absolute peace" – and that articulation's incontestable truth ("But didn't you set her crib on fire?") are pleasurably called into play.

Given this tacit mandate to have the film always attempt to perform or work through both thematically and structurally some of the topics Derrida's work interrogates, the problem of introducing Derrida as a biographical subject to audiences was one we struggled with for a considerable length of time. As Derrida's corpus is, in large part, a critique of certain prevailing conceptualizations of biography and autobiography, it would have been at the very least bizarre for us to present a cinematic narrative of his life in a way that reproduced uncritically the very structures his life's work was intent on examining. Kirby insightfully suggested that we look to already existing media clips to present the necessary introductory information, and we then came up with the idea of cutting them together in a montage. In this way, we were able to present the necessary rudimentary information about Derrida without our having to take responsibility as the source of this information, or ourselves authorize the claims being made about him and his stature. By delivering this information in this manner (as a representation of others' assertions), we were able to not only introduce our subject, but also point to issues of media, and mediation – issues broached and referenced in other ways throughout our film - and so again answer to our desire to have scenes within the film operate on multiple levels simultaneously.[5]

One particular sequence of footage especially challenged us with regard to our ambitions: the scene in which

we see Derrida walking through the streets of Paris. As evinced throughout our film, Derrida was, if nothing else, extraordinarily consistent in his feelings of ambivalence vis-a-vis all media surveillance, and so, on several occasions, he granted us access to film him only at the very last minute when we'd wholly not anticipated having such an opportunity. Once when I thought we'd concluded a shoot in his office at the Ecole des Hautes Etudes en Sciences Sociales in Paris on the Boulevard Raspail, he said to us, "So you will follow me?" He was preparing to leave his office and walk to a lecture hall several blocks away, but we had no idea we'd be invited along to film him in public during this walk (normally he didn't like having crews follow him about in public. It made him very uncomfortable, self conscious and embarrassed). Knowing better than to turn down an opportunity to shoot one's subject, but also knowing that we hadn't the proper camera equipment, insurance coverage, city permits or traffic clearance to execute this shoot successfully, we of course immediately said "but of course," as if that had been our plan all along. Hervé Cohen, our French production coordinator, drove his car with Kirsten Johnson, our camerawoman, precariously hanging out the window and Pascal Dupres, our sound man, attempting to direct Hervé so that he could drive alongside Derrida as he hastily strode through the streets of Paris without the whole crew perishing in an unfortunate traffic accident.

When we got back to the States, a cursory glance at the footage made me realize that we'd acquired (seemingly by accident) some extraordinary images – one couldn't have hired an actor to look more like an extremely glam French philosopher walking through the streets of Paris. Kirsten had somehow captured what most camera crews could only produce with hours of time, thought, lighting and preparation. The problem, though, then became how to use this oddly iconic and potent shot.

Kirby ingeniously decided to sync up the footage with a voiceover sonorously reciting a patter of mildly salacious and odd biographical facts – a sequence we came to affectionately refer to as the "National Enquirer montage." We hoped this incessant and oddly enigmatic stream of loaded anecdotes would at once undercut and highlight the fetishistic aspect of the shot, acting as a sort of modest send up of the insatiable cult of celebrity and referencing the voyeuristic aspect of the act that we, as an audience, all engage in when watching a cinematic portrait. The pairing would also playfully reference this issue of the anecdote that our film was thematically addressing – what is it one actually 'knows' when one thinks they know something about someone's private life?

Credit need also be given to Kirby for the idea to take excerpts from Derrida's writing and read them over non-narrative footage. For at least two years (!) Kirby had asked me to present him with a list of quotations to attempt

to use in the film. And for two years, I had assiduously dodged this request, not from sloth and indolence, but rather from an informed sense that it was impossible to extract pieces of Derrida's writing from their context without doing the work a tremendous disservice and injustice. Derrida's arguments are so imbricated, rich and dense that they do not lend themselves easily to extrication or reduction. Exasperated, Kirby decided one day to give up waiting for me and simply set about excerpting the work himself. In his own reading of Derrida's writings, he'd shrewdly noticed that often the start and endings of his essays have a more loaded amount of rhetorical drama, pathos and flourish, as well as some more conventional narrative elements, and so Kirby set about looking for openings or closings that he thought had both a profound poetic and theoretical resonance. I believe Kirby's not being an academic helped him read the texts in a different way, and freed him from some of the more reverential institutional preconceptions that haunted and to some degree paralyzed me when I approached Derrida's written works.

Once Kirby had selected his excerpts, he went through the footage both by himself (and later with our editor Matt Clarke) and found various scenic tracking shots and verité images that he thought might work well when placed in concordance with the quotes. He paired them together, recorded his own voice reading the quotes,

and then called me up and asked me to come to the cutting room to see what he had done.

I came in not knowing at all what to expect and was, I remember quite frankly, rather stunned. I thought that the cuts all somehow worked, each in their own way, and I was extraordinarily surprised. The excerpts Kirby had selected were strangely moving, and even though they had been wrenched from their context in Derrida's argument, I felt they still worked in their own odd and ineffably poetic way. And even if audiences didn't comprehend them all fully, they would at least be able to grasp something of their power and profundity – and that something was hardly nothing. Once we realized this technique formed a powerful cinematic conceit, we started inserting the quotes strategically throughout the film, using them to provide a certain anchor, ballast, and element of poetic flow and theoretical density to the surrounding material.[6]

As with the excerpts, our inclusion of the more humorous verité footage was more definitively and strategically placed in the cut somewhat late in the game. Kirby is a huge believer in test screenings, and we'd had several at various friends' homes that had met rather mixed responses. At some point after a particularly solemn audience response to an assembly of footage, Kathryn and I decided to go through all the footage and hunt for all the humorous moments, anecdotal or otherwise. Then we began to strategically place these moments throughout the

film to both provide much needed relief as well as further shore up and enrich whichever thematic moment was being explored (e.g., And so the burning crib quip was placed in the 'love' sequence; the Seinfeld comment used to cap the more somber 'political' South Africa sequence).

Once, in passing, Derrida had said to me that he thought of his work as being marked throughout by "un éclat de rire" ("a burst of laughter"). That comment stayed with me and to some extent informed our employment of humor in the film. Derrida's work is certainly witty if not overtly funny at times, and the discreet use of humor in the film was meant to pay homage to that fact. For it's not simply happenstance that Derrida employs humor in his own writing nor is it of only incidental significance that he offhandedly described his writing to me as being traversed or haunted throughout by a somewhat infectious or uncontrolled 'burst of laughter'. Derrida's affection for, and employment of, jokes and humor in his writing is, in part, due to the fact that jokes themselves operate as compact allegories for many of the very issues Derrida's work is intent on exploring in other arenas. That is to say, jokes are theoretically interesting linguistic constructs in that they quite overtly operate and depend upon the exploitation of a complex and sophisticated linguistic playing field. For a joke to register as funny, things described within it are not what they seem, or are not put forth to be understood only on a literal level – puns, double enten-

dres, irony, sarcasm, etc. all succeed thanks to a discordance between levels of intent and meaning. And it is the very play of this space/discordance/disjunction that generates the laugh, the pleasure. As jokes overtly exploit and foreground this polysemy that language inevitably offers, they are a nice figure or allegory for the type of more universal linguistic play that Derrida's writing is intent on examining, and to some extent, championing. And so, it was significant for us, not only strategically, but also theoretically, to have the film be funny.

I remember as well that Kirby and I were surprised to learn during one of our last filmed interviews with Jacques, that he comes from a family of veritable card-sharks. It's even apparently family lore that his mother once somewhat recklessly delayed a trip to the delivery room in order to properly finish playing out one particularly complicated hand. Again, this ostensibly incidental comment stuck with me for several reasons since it led me to reflect on the various ways card games – poker in particular – could be thought of in terms of effecting/affecting Derrida's theoretical work. For example, the game of poker relies on acts of dissimulation or bluffing, which – analogous to the workings of jokes – requires a juggling of issues of truth and intent. Poker also demands the continual negotiation of acts of strategy, contingency, necessity and chance; acts whose elements Derrida's work throughout is intent on examining (think again back on his 'le futur' and

'l'avenir' distinction).

Documentary filmmaking, verité style, likewise, can be viewed like a card game in that, the skill, to a large extent, comes in playing the hand you're dealt. That is, if one embarks, as we had, on an unscripted project, one needs to work with the footage acquired, and that limitation, to a great degree, invariably dictates/necessitates the editorial choices one makes. It was never my, or for that matter, our intention (once Kirby had joined the project), to make a film which referenced our own act of filmmaking. To me, it seemed like that self reflexive angle had already been fairly well played out and mined in film since the 60's and there was no need to revisit that issue again at this time. Likewise, I had never considered that I, as a character, would in any way appear 'in' the film a là a Nick Broomfield or Michael Moore. It had not even crossed my mind as being of interest or a possibility, as what was of import and interest to me – as well pretty much anyone who'd be watching the film – was Jacques Derrida and pretty much Jacques Derrida alone. And so, for the first four principle shoots there was never a camera on me or the film crew. Quite the contrary, Kirsten strove to keep me out of the frame if I ever threatened to appear within it.

However, once we started working with the material it became increasingly apparent that the self-referential angle would have to be addressed in some way since Derrida could not help but call attention to and reference the filmmaking process at any and all given opportunities. Pointing a camera at Jacques pretty much was like throwing chum to a shark – he couldn't refrain from in some way calling attention to the technological machinations. As an increasing amount of the footage began to inevitably refer to this fact, Kirby and I ultimately realized that there was in fact no way to avoid actually taking it up or, for that matter, even embracing it as a structural element of the film. In addition, since Jacques playfully sparred with me on camera throughout the film, and since our filmmaker/ subject relationship seemed to also nicely reflect and comment on certain prominent and fundamental themes in Jacques' work (e.g., issues of supplementarity, authorship, translation, signature, parasite/host relations), Kirby and I decided, after careful deliberation, to reference the filmmaker/ subject relationship in our film in both subtle and overt ways. This is how I came to figure, ever so slightly, as a character in the film – albeit a figure only ever shown in silhouette or partially obscured, but still included as a figure for the filmmaker in the film.

Once we decided that we were going to exploit/ explore this dimension, we began planning our subsequent shoots with an eye towards its inclusion (shooting scenes with multiple cameras, including crew shots in the frame, etc.). I also realized that despite our numerous attempts to secure a professional voice to read aloud the excerpts from Derrida's written work in the film,[7] it seemed most appropriate that the voice reading the excerpts of Derrida's work in the film literally be the voice of one of the filmmakers for I felt that this choice would further play out allegorically a dimension explicitly raised in Derrida's improvisation on the Echo and Narcissus myth. That is: we as filmmakers are condemned to only use Jacques' words – but in selecting and editing those words, we, a là Echo, to large degree, make them our own. To further extend this metaphor, the excerpts cited in the film are Derrida's words, but in cutting them and reading them aloud ourselves, we, again like Echo, appropriate them and make them (in some sense) our own.

Conversely, elements we'd assumed we'd include in the film completely fell by the wayside once we started working with the footage. We'd shot dozens of hours of interviews with colleagues, students and friends of Derrida thinking we might somehow work in this type of secondary source material. But once we started editing and inserting some of this material into cuts, we found it didn't at all play as we had hoped and that our portrait of Derrida was stronger if it was presented undiluted – that is without referring to the supervening authority of secondary opinions. While these interviews were all completely fascinating in their own right, we found that audiences were still most drawn to and compelled by the first person footage of Jacques, and that the film was stronger if we presented him without these adjudicating commentaries.

*

I'm often asked if this is the film I would have wanted to make, or if I've any regrets. Well, it might sound obvious, but in many ways I wish I knew everything I know now when I'd started making the film. If I'd had a better sense of the film's structure and nature from the outset, I think we would have been able to acquire even stronger footage. I also wish that at times personal circumstances hadn't prevented my going on certain shoots to which Jacques had graciously extended to me an invitation. And I wish that the film could have signaled a bit less obliquely the political import of Jacques work – for it is this political import which compelled me to make this film. (While that element is in the film, I am not sure if it is represented in the way I would most have liked it to be; and given more time, money, and the wisdom and clarity afforded by hindsight, this might have been an area I would have liked to have had the time to further work on in the film.)

As far as what I've been happy with, well I've been pleased and surprised that the film has succeeded to the extent it has, and that global audiences have responded to it with such pleasure, curiosity and interest. Kirby and I intentionally strove to make a film that would have the ability to appeal to a wide range of audiences – both those familiar with Derrida's work, as well as those who

had never heard of him - and we were both gratified to see that this was somehow achieved. Also, in this age of sound bites, and the ever accelerating proliferation and embrace of reductive inflammatory rhetoric in political and news arenas, it's been gratifying to see that the public has shown it is very much still interested in thinking at a different speed, and in examining the ways in which critical thinking can make a significant difference.[8] It was particularly striking that one of the most common questions we got during Q and A's following screenings was: "What work of his should I read?" We felt that if our film had somehow managed to repeatedly inspire that question, then maybe somehow we'd managed to do something right; and that maybe somehow, (just as he'd have wanted it), we'd managed to both breach and keep Jacques' impossible confidence.

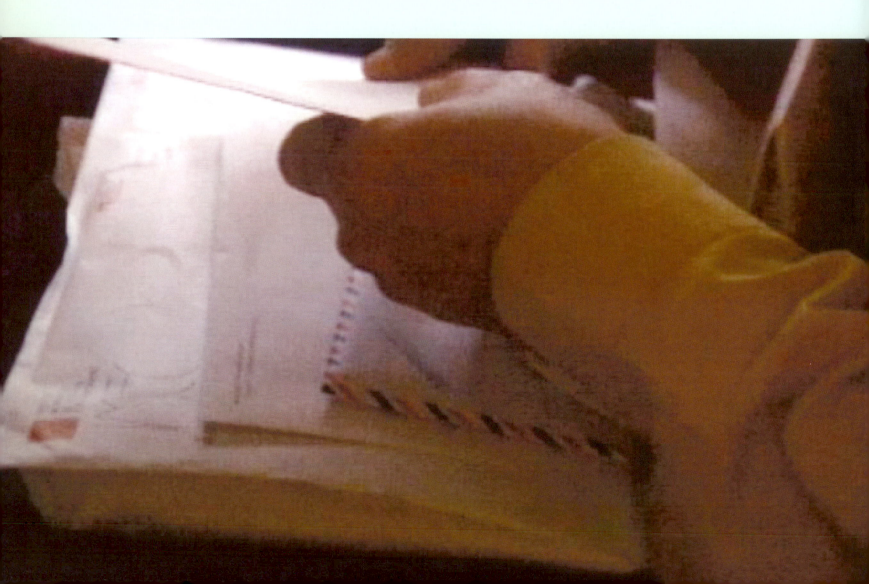

ENDNOTES

1.   Although I'd attended his seminars for several years at Yale as well as for a year at the Ecole Normale Superior when I lived in Paris in the 80's, I was fairly certain that he wouldn't have even the vaguest recollection of me as I was, at that time, a very intimidated grad student and had never spoken a word in his seminars.

2.   The long version of the short story being that when I went up to Jacques and asked him if he'd ever had a film made about him, he said that others had tried but not succeeded and that he really wasn't interested in that sort of thing, etc. I kept persisting and he finally said, (I think pretty much in an attempt to politely get rid of me) : "write me something…"
I went home and wrote a proposal and sent it off to him. After some further discussion, and then a long silence, I received one day in the mail a postcard from France that was, apart from the signature, completely indecipherable. His handwriting indubitably rivals the best of US physicians. Rather than face the incredibly awkward situation of calling him up and admitting that I had absolutely no idea what he'd written, I decided to assume via deduction that the postcard indicated his agreement (since I thought it was fair to infer that postcards are usually sent as a friendly gesture) and began writing grant proposals.

3.   For cinephile trivia fans, Dorn subsequently went on to edit, among other things, Chris Nolan's indie hit 'Momento' and Ridley Scott's 'Matchstick Men', films which deal in interesting ways with issues of temporality and interpretation (favorite Derridean topoi).

4.   Select examples of these more experimental approaches have been included on the DVD, under the 'deleted scenes' section.

5.   The idea of then intercutting these media statements with footage of Derrida preparing to leave the house to get his haircut came much later. I suggested this intercutting as a way to futher puncture or perforate the media statements as well as introduce an element of levity early on in the film.

6.   Special thanks need go to my sister Rosanne Ziering, as she, after having viewed several cuts, kept encouraging us to include more quotes as she strongly felt the quotes really were, in the end, somehow the heart of the movie.

7.   One of the more amusing ideas was to attempt to have David Duchovny of television's 'X Files' fame come on as the film's narrator. This wasn't an entirely insane idea as not only was Duchovny a fellow Yale grad student alumn (though I don't remember him ever taking Derrida's classes I did share some other classes with him at Yale) but I liked the fact that the 'X' of X files would cross reference the "X" of non-negation in Heiddeger's treatises. We could earn some celebrity cachet and a philosophical joke at one and the same time.

8.   Somewhat in keeping with both the preceding points, it was amusing and not a little gratifying to us that the film ironically hit theaters in the US at a time when our country had launched its war on Iraq and newspapers were replete with headlines trumpeting the need for Americans to now order Freedom fries and Freedom toast. It was at least nice to know that our film was coming out oddly enough at a bizarrely timely moment as an ambassador for a very different set of rhetorical and political principles, ones which demanded that one pay attention to and respect difference and complexity rather than feel threatened by it.

Kirby Dick

Resting on the Edge
of An Impossible Confidence

I first began working on *Derrida* shortly after completing *Sick: The Life and Death of Bob Flanagan, Supermasochist.* That film, also a documentary, was about the notorious and influential Los Angeles performance artist and writer Bob Flanagan, who was born with cystic fibrosis and was an extreme masochist. Throughout the making of *Sick,* I thought a great deal about the interplay between an artist's life and their work. So when I was presented with the opportunity to make a film about Jacques Derrida, I was intrigued, especially because of the way in which Derrida's writings often referenced this same interplay. I was also drawn to the project because I had read a great deal of one of Derrida's contemporaries, Jacques Lacan, and was interested in directly engaging theory, especially French theory, as the subject of a film.

While both films are centered on the personality and thought of a single subject, the two subjects could not have been more different. Throughout filming, Bob was extremely open about his personal, medical, and sexual experiences – which was consistent with the extremely direct autobiographical nature of his work. Derrida, on the other hand, with his southern Mediterranean gentility, remained very guarded about his personal life throughout the filming process, although he did grant us greater access to his life than he had granted to any other journalist or filmmaker. It took some time for me to get used to working within this limitation, although I understood the many rea-sons Derrida preferred this arrangement. One of these reasons, of course, was the very contentious relationship he'd had with the media throughout his life, a media that had often vilified him and misrepresented his thought. His uneasiness was longstanding, as he explained to Amy Ziering Kofman in her first filmed interview with him in 1995.

Up until 1979, when I say that I was strict (in terms of allowing myself to be photographed), it was much more serious than that. I absolutely forbade all types of public photographs. I like photography and have nothing against it, but I forbade any and all publications of photographs of me. It's very complicated, but one reason among others for this is that I believe that what I've written on literature, and on writing, has sought – socially and politically – to defetishize the author, the author as he appears in the photographic code – that is to say, often as just a portrait or head shot on the back of a book. I find this first of all ridiculous, comical, and related to all the types of com-mercial things with which I'd like to break.

Then, in 1979, I organized, with friends, a colloquium to defend philosophy from political attacks by the French government. There was a huge debate at the Sorbonne in which I actively participated, and there were many journalists there. It's the law in France that when you speak in a public space under certain situations you can't control the taking of your image, and so there were pho-tos of me that appeared in French newspapers at that time. As soon as these photos were public and available

I realized I could no longer enforce the interdiction, and so I let things go.

Derrida's ambivalence toward the media was more than theoretical - it was personal as well. Derrida was always very uncomfortable looking at his own image. Many people share this discomfort, but for Derrida it was exceptional – certainly in comparison to any other documentary subject I have worked with. This became evident to me one afternoon in Laguna Beach, California in August of 1999 when Amy and I met him to discuss an upcoming shoot. At this meeting, Amy presented Derrida with several extraordinary photos that her husband, Gil Kofman, had taken of him overlooking the California coast in which he looked vibrant, rugged, and appealing. Nonetheless, Derrida found fault with his appearance, and was unable to acknowledge how photogenic he was.

Throughout the making of the film, Derrida repeatedly commented on how difficult it was for him to look at any images of himself. In 1995, in the same interview quoted above, Derrida observed, "I have a very complicated rapport with my image. There is a mixture of, how should I say this, a narcissistic horror – I don't like my image." And three years later, after watching footage of himself speaking at a conference on biography at New York University, Derrida responded: "I hate to see and hear myself speak – especially in English, but also in French. My face, my mouth, it's a horrifying spectacle…If I were to see a lot of footage like this, I wouldn't be able to teach anymore." For Amy and I, this was compelling territory. Our subject, who had developed a rigorous theoretical position from which to critique the media and processes of representation, was also someone who was unable to comfortably view a representation of his own face. Derrida's conflicted relationship to his own image, combined with his critique of image making itself, generated a complex interplay between his personal anxieties and his theoretical analysis throughout much of the film.

Amy first mentioned to me that she had begun shooting a film about Derrida at a pre-release screening of *Sick* in 1996. As we began discussing the project, I was impressed with her ambition to find a cinematic way to let his theory inform the structure and style of the film, rather than make a standard biopic or present a simple explanation of his work. Over the following year, I reviewed much of the footage she had shot of Derrida in both the U.S. and France, and I found it quite remarkable. I was particularly struck by an interview with Derrida in which he seemed unusually relaxed and forthcoming. I was also intrigued by the hours of cinema verité style footage that her crew had shot of Derrida. This material, which included footage of him eating, talking on the phone, having breakfast with his wife, and looking for his keys in

the morning, offered a strangely captivating view into his quotidian life.

How did Amy manage to gain this kind of access to someone who was so guarded about his personal life? I think in part it was the result of a mutual naiveté between director and subject. Generally, a person of Derrida's stature is too busy and too wary to allow a camera into his home for such extended periods of time. But because this was the first film Amy directed, she audaciously asked for much more than another filmmaker might ask of a subject like Derrida: to spend several days following him with a camera crew. While it's true that documentary crews often spend days and occasionally weeks with a subject, it's rare that a subject of Derrida's stature is filmed in such a manner.[1] But Derrida, who, surprisingly, had not yet had a documentary made about him, assumed that the omnipresence of a film crew was not atypical and so agreed to her request.

This kind of undefined relationship between a documentary filmmaker and subject is not unusual. Unlike journalism, where there exists a set of ethics for how a journalist relates to his subject, the nature of the interaction between a documentary filmmaker and subject is almost entirely decided between the two of them, without reference to any established convention. (I know of no published rules of ethics for the profession that are considered standard.) A filmmaker can ask for as much

as they like, and a subject can offer as much or as little as they choose, and either can keep or break their arrangements as they see fit. This is one of the reasons verité documentaries are so fascinating. Each relationship between a filmmaker and subject is an open-ended undertaking based on an imprecise understanding, and the film is a record of the exploration of the limits of that understanding.

In addition to Amy and Derrida's mutual naiveté, there was another reason that Derrida offered us so much access to his personal life. Amy was able to forge a unique relationship with Derrida, one based upon an extensive knowledge of his work, genuine respect for him personally, and an unpredictable and disarming informality. As a result, she was able to elicit a much more personable response from him than many of his previous interlocutors, who often related to him with much more deference.

Most relationships between a documentary filmmaker and subject are at times a contest of wills. Our relationship with Derrida was no different, although he did have more control over the final product than most documentary subjects. In 1995, before shooting began, Derrida had added a handwritten clause to the contractual release of his image that gave him the right to view the film before it was exhibited, and to excise any scene or footage he wished. Few documentary filmmakers ever

agree to give a subject this kind of power, and for good reason. If a subject doesn't like the finished film, they can demand changes that compel the filmmaker to edit for months longer, and that may ultimately undercut the coherence and ambition of the film.

But giving up editorial control also brings some real advantages to the filmmaker. When filming begins, nearly every subject is concerned that the footage might be edited in a way they would object to. Knowing they have control over what will be seen reduces that anxiety and allows them to be more spontaneous. Moreover, if a subject has control, they will allow intimate or uncomfortable scenes to be filmed even if they never intend to agree to the use of those scenes in the film. As filming proceeds, however, a trust usually builds between a filmmaker and subject. Based on that trust, a subject often becomes more amenable to the inclusion of those scenes, especially by the time the film is being edited. But if the subject hadn't been granted the right during filming to later remove those scenes, the filmmaker would never have been given the opportunity to shoot them in the first place, and so, ultimately, the filmmaker would end up with much less material to work with.

Ceding editorial control is also a gesture that concretely demonstrates the filmmaker's desire that the subject's perspective will be an essential part of the film. But there is a unique dynamic that accompanies this understanding, a dynamic that neither the filmmaker nor the subject is fully aware of or has command over. By giving up control the filmmaker is, to some degree, giving up an element of authorship. In a way, the filmmaker is giving a gift to the subject, a gift the subject can receive only by implicitly agreeing to allow scenes to be filmed that they might want to excise later. By accepting editorial control, the subject unwittingly incurs an obligation to allow at least some objectionable scenes to be filmed. This dynamic is pervasive, and exists whenever the camera is rolling. It becomes an open-ended demand on the subject that the subject must then somehow respond to, otherwise they would not be fulfilling their part of the implicit understanding. In this arrangement, at every moment of the project, the filmmaker is in the position of being absolutely generous, a generosity that continually compels the subject to respond in a way that can always only be inadequate. The subject can never give enough to the filmmaker, because the filmmaker has given the subject everything that can be given – that is – control over the film. There are many other dynamics at play between filmmaker and subject, of course, but because the effect of this dynamic is rarely consciously considered or analyzed, it can have a powerful influence on the making of the film.

The first major shoot Amy and I undertook together was during one of Derrida's annual visits to the University

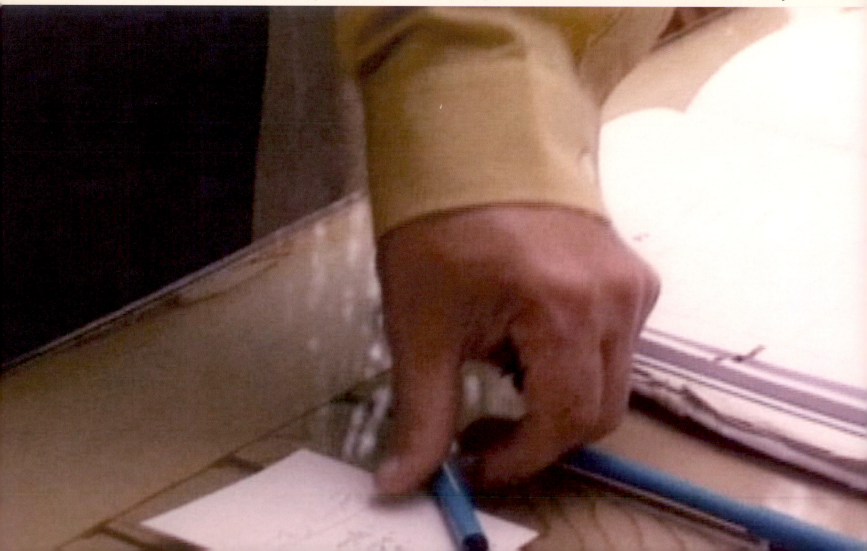

of California at Irvine, where, from 1987 through 2003, he had lectured and taught a graduate seminar course. We then conducted the film's second major interview with Derrida at his home in Laguna Beach, California, which the university had rented for him during his one month teaching stint at the school. For that interview we decided to focus on issues related to filmmaking, including Derrida's expectations, anxieties, and reflections about the making of this film, before asking him to speak about his more recent writing. (For this interview and all subsequent interviews, Amy and I together prepared the questions for Derrida in advance. Amy then asked the questions because she had the more established relationship with him.)

Even though Amy had a uniquely casual rapport with Derrida, he still had managed to maintain a kind of formality on camera, especially while he was being interviewed. To counter this, we began shooting him at all times with a second smaller digital video camera. Amy and I directed this hand-held camera to begin filming from the moment we met Derrida at his house in Laguna. Often operated by Gil Kofman, this camera continued to film throughout the production process – covering not only the primary interview, but also all of the interactions that were taking place with him throughout the crew set up, breakdown, and departure. I've found from *Sick* and other films I've made[2] that, in addition to capturing the crew and production process of the film, this kind of small camera often shows the subject in a more casual and personable way, especially in those moments immediately following the completion of an interview. The subject's relationship to the primary camera can be quite formal, in large part because of the amount of time devoted to framing and lighting prior to beginning an interview. When the interview is officially over and that camera is turned off, the subject finally relaxes and begins to interact much more casually with the interviewer and crew, often elaborating on previous answers. Frequently the subject will speak about things he was unwilling to say to the primary camera, even though he is aware a second camera is still shooting.

This dynamic first became evident when we took a break from the Laguna Beach interview, and, with our secondary camera continuing to shoot, showed Derrida footage of him and his wife that Amy had shot in 1995. Presented to him with the informality of home movies, our intent was not only to draw out his personal reaction to this intimate material but also to introduce into our film the problem of temporality in documentary filmmaking. Although most major documentaries take many years to complete (ours took nearly seven), filmmakers usually efface this temporality. Rather, the time over which the film was shot is presented within the film as a comprehensible linear narrative, and the editing process is rarely referenced. In *Derrida*, however, this temporality is foregrounded. At one point in our film, we see Derrida watching footage of an interview with him and his wife that was shot several years earlier. Later in the film, we see him watching himself on a video monitor watching the footage of that interview. By including these moments, we call attention to the fact that the process of making a film is always a part of the completed film and that a subject's ongoing and developing interaction with the filmmaking process is a part of the film as well.

These issues of temporality were further complicated and made more personal by seeing them filtered through Derrida's memory. In one moment in the film, as he's watching himself and his wife Marguerite eat breakfast together, he admits to being touched by seeing this intimate moment of his life that he no longer has any memory of. In another instance, while viewing an interview with Marguerite and himself in which they both answer and avoid answering Amy's question about the beginning of their relationship, Derrida seems genuinely moved by what remains unspoken, and observes that he and Marguerite are "resting on the edge of an impossible confidence." It is at these moments, when Derrida is observing the footage of himself with Marguerite, watching as they interact in silence or together refuse to speak, that one gains an unexpectedly intimate sense of their relationship.

"Resting on the edge of an impossible confidence" is perhaps a good way to describe a documentary filmmaker's relationship to their subject. Over the years of working on the film, Amy and I learned much more about Derrida's personal life than we ever intended to make a part of the film. Yet one of the themes of this film, as articulated by Derrida early on, is the importance of not effacing the personal biography from a consideration of a writer's work. Nonetheless, there is at least one aspect of Derrida's life that we didn't include. Out of deference to Derrida, we decided not to present his sexual life in any way that might make him uncomfortable. (This was a substantial change in approach for me. The subject of my previous film, Bob Flanagan, had made it a practice to respond as forthrightly as possible to any question about his sex life, no matter how personal or graphic it might be.) However, near the end of filming, it was Derrida himself who brought up the subject, at the end of our final interview with him in Paris, 2000.

Amy: If you were to watch a documentary about a philosopher – Heidegger, Kant or Hegel, what would you like to see in it?

Derrida: Their sex lives...I'd love to hear about something they refuse to talk about. Why do philosophers present themselves asexually in their work? Why have

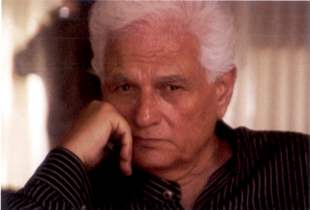

they erased their private lives from their work? Or never talked about anything personal? There is nothing more important in their private life than love…

Amy: And do you think you would want people to ask you such a question?

Derrida: Yes, I never said I'd respond to such a question but…in my texts there are already many things that reference this. I disguise things - but I don't do so in the same way as the other philosophers you've named.

One of the texts that Derrida is referencing here is The Post Card, which, of all his books, contains the most extensive references to his sex life. In that book, Derrida created a semi-fictional/semi-autobiographical character, offering an intriguing insight into his personal life, especially in the descriptions of that character's relationship with his lover. At one point during editing I became interested in incorporating these characters into the film, and juxtaposed a voiceover reading of Derrida's intimate first person description of their interactions with images of him alone in his home. The result was startlingly engaging, but unfortunately not in keeping with the tone of the rest of our film. We did, however, eventually use a number of excerpts from The Post Card in the scene in which a list of provocative biographical "facts" about Derrida is read. This list is presented straightfor-

wardly, as if all the facts are true, and, in fact, most are. But all we can know for certain about the excerpts we cite from this text is that they "happened" to the semi-fictional character of Derrida in The Post Card (e.g., that he received a phone call one night from someone claiming to be "Martini" Heidegger). By using his semi-autobiographical/ semi-fictional texts as source, we were able to add one more twist to this play of fiction and fact by suggesting that events that Derrida had presented as ambiguously fictional were ones he actually had experienced.

One particularly intriguing approach to incorporating sexuality into the film came during an interview with Richard Rand, one of the English co-translators of Glas. In response to a question about how he might imagine making a film on Derrida, Rand proposed that the film be fictional, and spontaneously came up with a complex film scenario:

> I would let the movie be about a woman, who would be the figure of Jacques Derrida, simply because Jacques is a man. She would be a passionate woman, and the film would cover much of the lifespan of this heroine. Let us allow that she has many lovers. They would all fall in love with her, and she would maintain a relationship with each, such that each would feel completely singled out. This would continue over the years: some relationships would simply end; some would weave in

and out. To make this an interesting movie, there would have to be a principle of fidelity finally holding the thing together. (One of the lovers might be me, but I do not see myself as the one to whom my heroine would be the most faithful.)

The ending would have to be ever so slightly tendentious. It would end up that one man counts more than any other man, and when it happens you would know that it happens. The allegorical take would be that my heroine is capable of infinite attention to a variety of partners yet one is more singular and to him she'd be more faithful. Let the title be the name of the heroine. That's how I would do it - and I think justice could be done, in a funny way, even in Hollywood. And perhaps Vanessa Redgrave could play Jacques Derrida.

Although we didn't use Rand's response in the final edit, the question we put to him points to the approach Amy and I took to the film. The process of making the film was in many ways the search for a form. Rather than have that form be set in advance, we chose to have it be a response to the interaction between the filmmakers and the subject, and to the material that developed from that interaction. We felt this particularly appropriate for a film about Derrida, because of the unusual interplay between form and content in his writing. Interestingly, the nature of his writing also produced a curious restraint as well. Because his work has a strong

polemical tone, it seems to demand that any writing or text about his work conform to the precepts he puts forth. More than with any other subject I've made a documentary about, there was an underlying demand that the film be made in the style of the subject's work. Specifically, this demand, which emanated from audiences, critics, and even from Amy and me, was that our film (indeed any film) about Derrida be "Derridean." Or, to put it another way, our film should "do Derrida to Derrida."

There has also been a demand, from some, that the film address the various controversies surrounding Derrida and his career. Early on in the project, Amy and I discussed how we might focus on these controversies, and, in an early cut, we included a scene that examined the "Cambridge Affair",[3] and his response to it. Ultimately we chose, for many reasons, to not include these disputes. We felt that by highlighting them we would be repeating one of the most common responses by the media to Derrida, which is to examine the reaction to his work rather than the work itself. However, I continue to be intrigued by the amount of antagonism elicited by his name and by the term "deconstruction". This antagonism often seemed to manifest itself to me in one especially peculiar way. Whenever I would mention to acquaintances that I was working on a film about Derrida, often their first response was "Isn't he dead?" The fact that so many

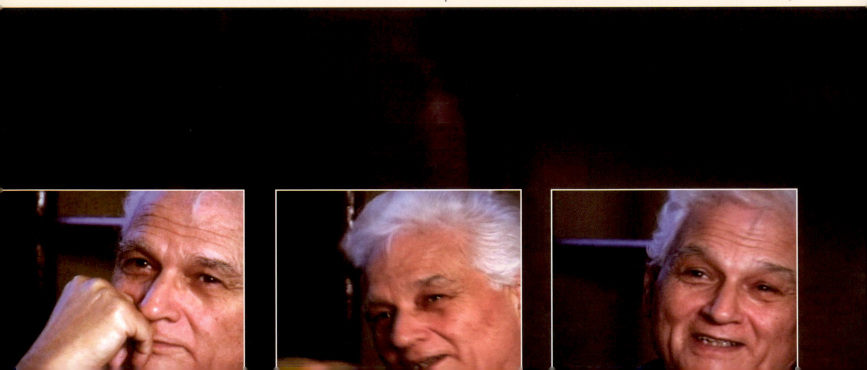

people would presume this suggested to me that there was an unconscious public desire for him to be dead, finally dead, perhaps so that we no longer would have to engage the difficulty and ambition of his work. In an interview with Amy, which I regret not finding a way to use in the film, Derrida offers some insight into his subconscious anxieties surrounding the contentious reception of his work:

I'm not argumentative, but it's true that deconstructive gestures often have the appearance of destabilizing, worrying, or antagonizing others. Each time I make this gesture, I have a moment of fear - but it doesn't occur at the moment of when I am writing. When I write, there is a force stronger than myself that compels me to write what I write, whatever the consequences. So nothing intimidates me when I write.

But when I'm falling asleep, there is a moment, in this state of half sleep, when all of a sudden what I'm doing frightens me. And I'll say to myself, "You are crazy to write this… You are crazy to criticize this person, to contest this authority, be it a textual authority, a personal authority, or an institutional authority – and I feel a sort of subconscious panic.

I compare this panic to that of a child who does something shameful, and then dreams, as Freud has noted, that he is walking in public naked. And he is afraid because everyone sees that he is naked. In this state of half sleep

I have the feeling that I'm doing something criminal, shameful, and inadmissible that I shouldn't have done. The order that is implied here is for me to stop what I'm doing, to burn my papers – that what I'm doing is inadmissible. But when I wake up, it's over. So when I'm awake, conscious, at work, I am, in a certain way, more unconscious than when I am in this state of half sleep. In this state of half sleep there is a certain vigilance which tells me the truth, that sees that what I'm doing is grave. But when I am awake and working this vigilance is asleep.

Throughout the film, Derrida references the relationship between image making and death. Inevitably the idea of death is present in the making of any documentary, especially those with a biographical focus. In *Sick*, the subject's death was specifically incorporated into the film's actual production schedule. For years Bob Flanagan's work had focused on his disease, cystic fibrosis, and his expected early death.[4] By the time I proposed making a film about him, he was in his early forties and was becoming increasingly ill. One of his few requirements for making the film was that I continue shooting the project up to and through his own death, regardless of when that might occur. (He eventually died two years after I began shooting.) So death is continually at play throughout *Sick*, and each moment Bob is on camera is a videotaped communication from Bob to audiences that he knew would only receive it after he died. In *Sick*, this relationship

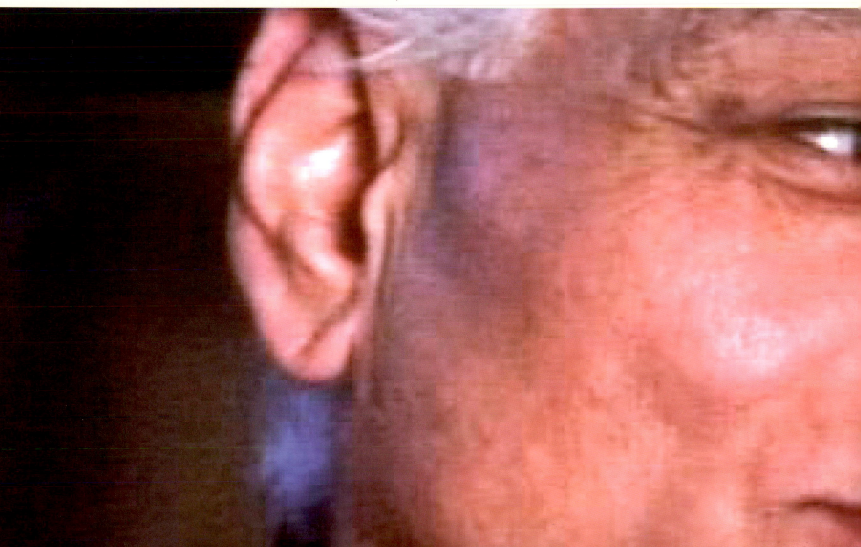

between image making and death is directly referenced at the very beginning of the film when Bob comically reads his own obituary, which he himself had composed and presented directly into the camera. Although Derrida has written extensively about death and its relationship to writing, his anxiety about death seemed to take on an especially personal tone around the making of our film. In our final interview with him in Laguna Beach, he discussed this anxiety and its symptoms:

> JD: In a sort of fantastic way, I often have the impression that I'll die in the next second. It's not a game, because it's very stressful, but it's something that I often make myself imagine. I play these kinds of movies for myself, where I see myself living in that last moment and then I see all the people who were around me saying: "We were just filming the movie in this Laguna Beach villa and he'd talked about this and that, and we'd talked about death. Right afterward, he had a heart attack." And I often have the image of being in a car accident - that's the scenario that is the most frequent and inevitable. It's compulsive. I think about it all the time, even at times when nothing is happening that could make me feel that this death is possible. But I nearly always take the necessary precautions so that if something were to happen, everything would be in order, there wouldn't be any loose papers.

> Amy: It's strange that you filter the view of your own death through the perspective and voices of others.

Why?

> JD: I don't have an answer for that other than I can't think about my death without thinking about who will be left after my death. I feel watched. Like right now. What am I doing? You're filming me. Even if I live to be very old, which I hope, these images will most likely live longer than I. So there will be people who can see these images when I'm dead. That's inscribed in the structure of what we're doing. Death is here. We are filming someone who we know will die before the archive.

When the film was released in North America and Europe, Derrida was generous in his support. But it is always difficult for a documentary subject to relate to a film about him/herself, and I am certain this was so with Derrida. The uneasiness he would inevitably feel when gazing at a photograph of himself certainly must have been considerably intensified whenever he watched himself on film for 90 minutes. But for documentary film subjects there is another difficulty, one that arises only after the film has been in release for several months. When a subject sees the film for the first time, they generally accept their portrayal, provided the film doesn't misrepresent them or isn't excessively critical. They may be uneasy about the way they look or what they say, or wish that the film presented other aspects of their lives, but they nonetheless see an aspect of themselves in the film that they feel is accurate. They understand that what is shown is only a partial representation of them, a character constructed by the filmmakers. It is no more an absolute depiction of themselves than a single photograph is a definitive representation of the way a person looks – considering that one's look is continually changing from moment to moment depending on mood, lighting, context, age etc.

When an audience watches the film, however, they see a refined cinematic presentation of the subject in personal and often very dramatic situations. Based on this condensed intimacy, audiences feel as if they have come to personally know the subject over the course of watching the film. They presume that the character presented in the film is essentially identical to and fully interchangeable with the actual person. When one of these viewers, especially one who doesn't know the subject well, later meets the subject, they relate to him or her as the character they have seen on screen, a character which in actuality is nothing more than one filtered and very selective representation of the subject. A documentary film, then, creates a doppelganger of the subject in the public consciousness, one that haunts any interaction between the subject and anyone who has seen the film. For years after a film's release, the subject must contend with the presence of this doppelganger, until its effect finally subsides and other representations arise to take its place.

A doppelganger is created with any public presentation - a book, an interview, or a photograph - but I think its effect is most pervasive with documentary films because of the sense of intimacy and immediacy that the moving image generates. One of the first times Derrida had to publicly contend with this kind of doppelganger was on the evening of the film's theatrical premiere in New York, where he appeared in front of audiences after the film had been screened. He seemed very much aware of its presence, having been represented in many other contexts for several decades. So when asked what he thought of the film, his response was very much consistent with his character in the film:

> I love the film. What can I say? I know, given all the footage they have, another film would have been possible, perhaps a totally different film, perhaps a better one, I don't know, perhaps worse. My feeling is that it's done, it's irreversible, and I'm happy that it's been done. Let me put it that way because I don't want simply to make compliments and to say, "I love the film." If I were here to say, "I love the film," that would be ridiculous, because it's me, okay? I won't say I love the film. Narcissism is one of the subjects of the film, so "Narcissus loves the film" would then appear as a headline on a review of the film. All I can say is that I was very anxious about the result, during the years [it took to complete], and I have been reassured, let's say, to a large extent by what I saw.[5]

Just as Derrida must now contend with the existence of a virtual representation of himself, I too, as a filmmaker,

am engaged in an interaction with the virtual as well. One of my fascinations with making verité documentaries is the complexity of the relationship between myself and the subject, or rather between the two subjects and myself. For there are two – one is the actual subject, whom I get to know personally, and sometimes become very close to – and the other is the virtual subject, the one I manage to craft from whatever footage the real subject allows me to shoot. I am continually interacting with these two subjects, often at the same time. But in addition to my ongoing relationship with both of these subjects, there is also a deferred relationship with each, deferred through an audience, a future audience, one that will see the film, my love letter (for that is what all documentaries are), a letter which will be sent to both my real and virtual subjects via an audience. And though I want the real subject to like the film, in the end it isn't what is essential. Of course, if he or she doesn't like the film, it becomes personally less gratifying to present the film in public, but ultimately this is not what is most important to me. Nor is it essential that the audience like the film, although their response determines its success or failure, and my success or failure as well. Rather, the film is finally made for yet another virtual subject – not for the subject that I have created nor for the actual subject, but for the subject that I love, the subject I would most like to present the film to. Of course, there is no way for that virtual subject to see the film, to like or dis-

like the film, or to receive or respond to the film in any way. So, like Derrida, I too remain "resting on the edge of an impossible confidence", careful to tell only what I imagine this virtual subject would want me to say.

ENDNOTES

1.   Since the advent of reality programming, this type of documentary coverage has become more commonplace. As a genre, reality programming is already beginning to influence the way subjects relate to a documentary camera. This first became apparent to me when I made a film with a group of urban Los Angeles high school students. I was surprised that, rather than being suspicious about the presence of the camera, which I had always experienced with previous documentary subjects, including Derrida, the students instead embraced being filmed. For them, being represented in the media was empowering, because they believed that the media gave legitimacy and stature to whatever it chose to represent, regardless of the type of programming. Being excluded entirely by the media, and therefore having their lives and points of view effaced by society, was the usual state of affairs for them. They considered the effect of this effacement more insidious and damaging than the risk of being misrepresented by the media. Subjects from Derrida's generation, and even of the following generation, have not grown up with the same exposure to reality programming, and they remain much more wary of it. However, as the generation raised on reality programming matures, I suspect that it will become easier for documentary filmmakers to gain access to their subjects' personal lives, regardless of how accomplished their subjects may be.

2.   About a year and a half after beginning work on Derrida I began making another film, entitled Chain Camera, which made much more extensive use of small video cameras. For several years prior, I had been interested in working with footage that I "commissioned" but did not direct. With Chain Camera, I developed a process to generate that kind of footage. I arranged for ten students at a large, urban Los Angeles high school to each take a camera and film their lives for a week. At the end of the week, the students each gave their camera to another student, who in turn filmed his or her life for a week, before once again passing the camera on. Like chain letters, these cameras circulated throughout the school for an entire year. I worked with Matthew Clarke, the editor of Chain Camera, (and co-editor of Derrida) for over a year, editing the more than 700 hours of film that the students shot into a 90-minute film.

3.   In 1992 at Cambridge University, the granting of an honorary degree to Derrida provoked an impassioned debate among the dons. Twenty philosophers signed a letter to protest the award, maintaining, among other things, that Derrida's work was composed of "tricks and gimmicks similar to those of the Dadaists" (as if that was inherently an undesirable characteristic). The end result was the unusual step of putting the issue to a vote, which was settled by a 336-204 vote in Derrida's favor. On June 11, 1992 Cambridge bestowed the Honorary Degree on Jacques Derrida.

4.   One particularly sensational piece that Bob proposed but never realized was to have a video camera buried inside his coffin that could transmit images of his decomposing body to a gallery. Viewers in that gallery would have the option to flip a switch that would light the interior of the coffin and show the current state of decomposition of Bob's body. He also developed a variation on this idea in which the image inside the coffin would be transmitted via satellite so that it would be available for all to see over the Internet.

5.   Several weeks later after this screening, Amy called Derrida at his home in France and Marguerite, upon answering the phone, said "I hear you've made him into Clint Eastwood." When Amy did finally speak with Derrida he reported that, subsequent to the film's release, he was recognized with much greater frequency on the streets of New York. He commented that this development was quite strange for him since all his life he had been traveling the globe very anonymously, only occasionally being recognized in public when he went into bookstores.

DERRIDA

JANE DOE FILMS

Film to Text Adaptation by Gil Kofman

In general, I try to distinguish between what one calls the future and "l'avenir."

The future is that which – tomorrow, later, next century – will be.

But there is a future that refers to someone whose arival is totally unexpected.

Jackie, do you have your keys?

EXTERIOR. PARIS - DAY

A POV of the Seine and Parisian landscape glimpsed as if through a subway train window. As the images pass, we hear:

Derrida (in French):

DERRIDA (O.S.)
In general, I try to distinguish between what one calls the future and "l'avenir." The future is that which – tomorrow, later, next century – will be. There's a future that is predictable, programmed, scheduled, foreseeable. But there is a future, l'avenir (to come), which refers to someone who comes whose arrival is totally unexpected. For me, that is the real future. That which is totally unpredictable. The Other who comes without my being able to anticipate their arrival. So if there is a real future beyond this other known future, it's l'avenir in that it's the coming of the Other when I am completely unable to foresee their arrival.

Slowly the rush of landscape comes to a halt.

INTERIOR. DERRIDA'S HOME - RIS-ORANGIS, FRANCE - MORNING

Scenes alternate between footage of Derrida in his house in the morning intercut with News Footage documenting his reputation and renown.

Preoccupied, Derrida enters from an enclosed glass patio.

MARGUERITE (O.S.)
Jackie, do you have your keys?

DERRIDA
Yes, I have them.

He opens the hall closet and hangs a jacket.

CUT TO: CLOSE UP: POLISH NEWSCASTER

POLISH NEWSCASTER
This century has given us philosophers of highest caliber, notables like Husserl, Bergson, Wittgenstein, Heidegger, Ricoeur, and Levinas. It would seem that the list of the century's greatest men of thought would be closed. Who else could possibly compare to them? And yet, this list of great thinkers would not be complete without Jacques Derrida.

BACK TO: DERRIDA

He shuts closet and puts on his jacket. Turns to address camera.

DERRIDA
Forgive me for not even saying hello. It's a bit difficult…

This century has given us philosophers of the highest caliber...

CUT TO: ANOTHER BROADCASTER - FROM THE BBC

She speaks OVER a PHOTO of Derrida which DISSOVLES to the COVER of Derrida's seminal text, "WRITING AND DIFFERENCE."

BBC CORRESPONDENT (O.S)
Good Evening, later on tonight's late show we look at the French philosopher Jacques Derrida, founder of the post-structuralist mode of analysis known as deconstruction and internationally acknowledged by many as one of the most innovative and inspiring of contemporary philosophers.

BACK TO: DERRIDA

Still trying to exit his home. Now heading for the front door. Again he turns to Camera.

DERRIDA
Okay, I've got my keys. So you're going to follow me? When we get there, there's a garage, and I'll have to speak to someone at the hair salon about arranging to park your car.

MORE MEDIA - FROM BELGIUM

Derrida intently listening to the introduction.

BELGIAN NEWSCASTER
Born in El Biar, Algeria, Jacques Derrida's name is now known on five continents. He's a thinker of lightening thoughts whose work is like that of miners who work by exploding the beams supporting their shafts.

BACK TO: DERRIDA

…now getting into his car.

Again the Seine as seen through a moving car window.

Over this, as if written on water itself, OPENING CREDITS appear and disappear.

She sees everything but she is totally blind.

That's the image of the philosopher who falls into the well, while looking at the "star."

OPENING TITLE SEQUENCE

MUSIC COMPOSED BY
RYUICHI SAKAMOTO

EDITED BY
KIRBY DICK
MATTHEW CLARKE

ASSOCIATE PRODUCER
GIL KOFMAN

CAMERA
KIRSTEN JOHNSON

PRODUCER
AMY ZIERING KOFMAN

DIRECTED BY
KIRBY DICK
AMY ZIERING KOFMAN

DERRIDA

As the last OPENING CREDIT fades – a police siren SOUNDS in the distance marking the transition to:

EXT. NEW YORK CITY - AFTERNOON

Derrida and company – Professors Alan Chodolenko, Peggy Kamuf, Derrida advance toward us, preparing to cross the street.

ALAN CHODOLENKO
My theory is that Americans exist to the degree that they're being filmed or believe themselves to be filmed. This is their natural condition.

DERRIDA (re: Camera)
You see how Americanized I am.

As they cross the busy street – Camera Jolts.

DERRIDA (addressing CAMERAWOMAN)
Careful.

Derrida stops at median, waiting for a pause in traffic – pointing to Camerawoman.

DERRIDA
She sees everything around me but she is totally blind. That's the image of the philosopher who falls in the…(how do you say?) well, – while looking at the star. (pointing to himself)

All laugh. Then cross street.

INT. NEW YORK UNIVERSITY (NYU) - LOBBY - DAY

Derrida, still with colleagues, waits at an elevator.

DERRIDA (referring to Camera Crew):
I have these people around all the time, day and night, wherever I am.

WOMAN
It's like the Loud family.

DERRIDA
For two weeks now they have been constantly tracking me.

WOMAN
So are you getting used to it?

DERRIDA
Sometimes I forget, I just forget.

INT. NYU LECTURE - BIOGRAPHY CONFERENCE - DAY

DERRIDA
We should not neglect the fact that some biographies – written by people that have authority in the academy – finally invest this authority in a book, which for centuries, sometimes after the death of an author, represents the truth. The "truth". If someone interested in biography writes: "The Life and Works of Heidegger", and it's well documented, apparently consistent, and it's the only one, published under the authority of a good press, then Heidegger's image, Heidegger's life image is fixed and stabilized for centuries. That's why I would say that sometimes the one who reads a text by a philosopher, even for instance just one tiny paragraph, and interprets it in a rigorous, inventive and powerfully deciphering fashion, is more of a real biographer than the one who knows the whole story.

CUT TO: INT. LAGUNA BEACH HOUSE - CALIFORNIA - DAY

Derrida and one of the film's directors, Amy Ziering Kofman, (AZK) deliberating over what Derrida should wear for an upcoming interview.

DERRIDA
This is the blue jacket I have.

AZK
That's nice.

DERRIDA
But this doesn't fit with this... This is black and this is not blue, o.k. and I usually can't...

AZK
I know, we won't get your bottom half, can I just see it what it looks like, is that okay? I'm sorry to trouble you.

BACK TO: INT. NYU BIOGRAPHY CONFERENCE - CONTINUOUS

DERRIDA
As you know traditional philosophy excludes biography, considers biography as something external to philosophy. You remember Heidegger's statement about Aristotle....Heidegger once was asked, "What was the life of Aristotle?" What could we answer to the question "what was Aristotle's life?" Well the answer is very simple, "Aristotle was a philosopher", and the answer holds in one sentence: "He was born, he thought, and he died." And all the rest is pure anecdote.

CUT TO: EXT. PARIS - DAY

Derrida walking through streets of Paris alone, smoking a pipe.
Over this tracking shot we hear the Narrator (AZK) dispassionately listing a string of ostensibly biographical facts.

VOICEOVER
His Mother's grave is profaned.
His parents never read any of his books.
He cries out: "Mommy I'm scared" every night until she lets him sleep on a sofa near them.
One side of his face is paralyzed for three weeks leaving his eye open continuously unblinking.
His father composes his own death notice shortly before he dies of cancer.
He is expelled from school because he is Jewish.
He learns he was given a secret name, Eli, after the Jewish prophet Elijah that isn't on his birth certificate.
He fails his first entrance exam to the University.
He writes his first novel at age fifteen about the theft of a diary and blackmail for its return.
He pretends to learn Hebrew so as to read it without understanding it.
He is arrested and thrown in prison for 24 hours in Prague for transporting drugs which the authorities plant on him.
He receives a collect call from someone who identifies himself as Martini Heidegger.
He doesn't circumcise his sons greatly upsetting his Mother and Father.
As an adolescent, he dreams of becoming a professional soccer player.
He declines and offer from Marguerite Duras to play a part in one of her films.
He suffers from sleeplessness and nervous collapse from the overuse of sleeping tablets and amphetamines.
His older brother lives only seven days, dying just a year before he is born.

BACK TO: INT. NYU BIOGRAPHY CONFERENCE - LATER

DERRIDA
If classical philosophers usually avoid autobiography, it is because they think it's indecent. That is, a philosopher should not speak of himself as an empirical being. And this impoliteness, or this politeness is philosophy itself, in principle. So if we

Okay, I've got my keys. So you're going to follow me?

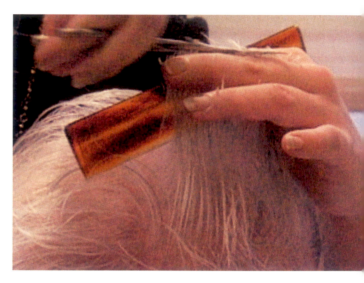

want to break with this philosophical axiom, this classical philosophical axiom, according to which a philosopher should not present himself or give in to autobiography, then we have to be indecent to some extent.

Close up: Fingers parting Derrida's white hair. Then scissors snipping.

We Are...

INT. HAIR SALON - RIS-ORANGIS - DAY

Slo-mo of scissors cutting and as the hair falls – We Hear:

VOICEOVER (AZK)
We no longer consider the biography of a philosopher as a set of empirical accidents that leaves one with a name that would then itself be offered up to philosophical reading, the only kind of reading held to be philosophically legitimate. Neither readings of philosophical systems nor external empirical readings have ever in themselves questioned the dynamics of that borderline between the work and the life, between the system and the subject of the system. This borderline is neither active nor passive, it's neither outside nor inside. It is most especially not a thin line, an invisible or indivisible trait that lies between the philosophy on the one hand, and the life of an author on the other. (THE EAR OF THE OTHER 1982).

On the Hair Salon's mirrored wall, Derrida is now multiplied and REVEALED in an infinite regression of mirrors – haircut almost all finished.

CUT TO: INT. NORTHWESTERN UNIVERSITY - DAY

Students surround Derrida to ask questions and introduce themselves.

STUDENT #1:
Listening to you speak just elucidated your texts just so much for me.

DERRIDA:
Thank you. Thank you.

STUDENT #1:
But I just wanted to meet you.

STUDENT #2:
I read one of your novels over the summer... I just wanted to hear you speak so I could understand it better.

STUDENT #3:
I started reading about negative theology and I was wondering if there was any connection between that and Hebrew Kabala?

DERRIDA:
There are a number of connections...
As Derrida responds, the Soundman fumbles to remove the small microphone from

I've already in a way started to respond to your question about deconstruction.

It is not an operation that supervenes afterwards from the outside...

Derrida's jacket. It takes a great deal of time and effort, as the Soundman finds to his dismay that he needs to remove the entire contents of Derrida's pocket in order to successfully extricate the mic – then next awkwardly realizes he has to now discreetly return the removed contents to Derrida's jacket pocket before exiting frame.

CUT TO: INT. DERRIDA'S HOME STUDY - PARIS - DAY

Flanked by books, Derrida is being interviewed by an Off-screen AZK.

AZK (O.S.)
You're very well known in the states for "deconstruction". Can you talk a little about the origin of that idea?

DERRIDA:
Before responding to this question, I want to make a preliminary remark on the completely artificial character of this situation. I don't know who's going to be watching this, but I want to underline rather than efface our surrounding technical conditions, and not feign a "naturality" which doesn't exist. I've already in a way started to respond to your question about deconstruction because one of the gestures of deconstruction is to not naturalize what isn't natural – to not assume that what is conditioned by history, institutions, or society is natural.

Derrida continues to talk – but it is now AZK's Voice we hear. She is reading from Derrida's – MEMOIRES FOR PAUL DE MAN.

VOICEOVER
The very condition of a deconstruction may be at work in the work, within the system to be deconstructed. It may already be located there, already at work. Not at the center, but in an eccentric center, in a corner whose eccentricity assures the solid concentration of the system, participating in the construction of what it, at the same time, threatens to deconstruct.

As the voiceover continues to narrate, slowly another IMAGE of Derrida preparing to begin teaching his class at the Ecole des Hautes Etudes en Sciences Sociale, gradually bleeds from under the existing initial image of Derrida responding to the interviewer's question. Both images appear simultaneously. Voiceover continues throughout.

VOICEOVER (CONT'D)
One might then be inclined to reach this conclusion: deconstruction is not an operation that supervenes afterwards, from the outside, one fine day. It is always already at work in the work. Since the destructive force of deconstruction is always already contained within the very architecture of the work, all one would finally have to do to be able to deconstruct, given this always already, is to do memory work. Yet since I want neither to accept or to reject a conclusion formulated in precisely these terms, let us leave this question suspended for the moment. (MEMOIRES FOR PAUL DE MAN 1986)

Gaining in strength and dominance – the Image of Derrida at his classroom desk, now fully replaces the original IMAGE of Derrida in his library at home. We Transition fully To…

So as an experiment,

we'll see what it's like to work for a moment

in the presence of these archiving machines.

I want to explain the presence of

and ask your permission for this film crew on my left.

This is a California film crew, by the way.

INT. ECOLE DES HAUTES ETUDES EN SCIENCES SOCIALES (EHESS) LECTURE - PARIS - DAY

Derrida begins to address the class. Derrida's wife, Marguerite, and close friend and colleague, Helene Cixous, sit side by side listening in the audience.

DERRIDA
I want to explain the presence of and ask for your permission for this film crew on my left. They'll be recording some images and I hope this occurs as imperceptibly as all the other recording devices we've become accustomed to. Recording devices, notably video or filmic ones, have been a topic of our seminar. On several occasions, we examined them in light of the example posed by the Rodney King verdict.
(pointing at CAMERA)
This is a California film crew, by the way. In that case we posed the question: What happens to the testimonial archive when one takes into account that the classic definition of testimony excludes the intervention of recording devices? So as an experiment we'll see what it's like to work for a moment in the presence of these archiving machines.

CUT TO: INT. DERRIDA'S HOME - RIS-ORANGIS - DAY

Close Up: FAX MACHINE – Derrida's signature visible in center of frame.

Angle On: Derrida on phone, in home office. We catch snatches of his conversation.

DERRIDA (talking on the phone):
Agnes called me yesterday to talk about the meeting... it's canceled? Yes,... yes.. well, that's not bad...

CUT TO: *Close-up on Derrida's hands, playing with two pens resting on a table.*
CUT TO: *Derrida descending attic stairs with a pile of books.*

DERRIDA'S VOICE
So, this is what you call cinema verité?

Now recharging his pipe in his den – addressing CAMERA directly.

DERRIDA
Everything is false. Almost, almost everything. I'm not really like this. First of all, I don't usually dress like this.

AZK (O.S.)
No?

DERRIDA
No, you must know that when I stay at home alone in the daytime, I don't get dressed. I stay in my pajamas and a bathrobe.

AZK (O.S.)
All day?

Everything is false.

First of all, I don't usually dress like this.

When I spend all day at home, I don't get dressed.

I stay in my pajamas and a bathrobe.

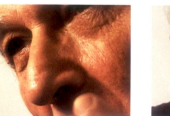

To go back to what we were saying earlier about seeing and touching,

what interests me about the eyes...

one can find one's childhood in the look of the eyes.

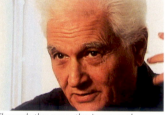

Hegel says that the eyes are the outer manifestation of the soul.

Through the eyes, the inner soul presents itself to the outside.

But it's very difficult to have an image of our own act of looking...

DERRRIDA

Yes until I leave the house. When I spend all the whole day at home, I don't get dressed.

VAROUS SHOTS of:

Derrida on phone, arranging papers in his glass-enclosed patio/office – as seen from across his backyard. As we watch, we hear AZK reading a passage from Derrida's DISSEMINATION:

VOICEOVER

Who is it that is addressing you? Since it is not an author, a narrator, or a deus ex machina it is a "I" that is both part of the spectacle and part of the audience. An "I" that, a bit like " you", undergoes its own incessant violent reinscription within the arithmetical machinery. An " I" that functioning as a pure passageway for operations of substitution is not some singular and irreplaceable existence, some subject or life. But only rather moves between life and death, between reality and fiction. An "I" that is a mere function or phantom. (DISSEMINATION 1972)

CUT TO: INT. STUDIO - BODY PARTS IMPROVIZATION #1 - PARIS - DAY

All IMPROV Segments are shot handheld. With Derrida floating against an over-exposed white background – and a variety of angles Jump Cut together from the perspectives of three different cameras. His thought and speech, however, are continuous.

DERRIDA – IMPROV #1

Let me think. To go back to what we were saying earlier about seeing and touching, about seeing and speaking, and seeing and touching…Instead of getting enmeshed in a profound meditation on sight which I've written about and discussed at length elsewhere, I'd like to say that what interests me about the eyes is that they are the part of the body that doesn't age. In other words, if one looks for one's childhood across all signs of aging in the body – the deterioration of musculature, the whitening of the hair, changes in height and weight – one can find one's childhood in the look of the eyes. And what's striking about this is that a man of my age keeps the exact same eyes that he had as a child. Hegel says that the eyes are the outer manifestation of the soul. Through the eyes, the inner soul presents itself to the outside. But I translate this thought as follows: That one's act of looking has no age. One's eyes are the same all of one's life. And I'll say something related to this about the subject of hands. In a book I just published, I spoke a lot about hands. I'm very interested in the hands of philosophers. I've written a text on the hands of Heidegger, which also references the hands of Kant, Husserl…So the hands of philosophers interest me a lot. And what they say about hands, and the privilege that's given to this part of the body. Keeping in mind that there's a history of the hand, the evolution of man, what we call the hominization of the animal, occurs via the transformation of the hand. I think that it's not the body of the hand that stays the same, the hand changes from childhood to old age. It is the eyes and hands that are the sites of recognition, the signs through which one identifies the Other. To return to the question of narcissism, they are, paradoxically, the parts that we see the least easily. We can look in a mirror and see ourselves and have a reasonably accurate sense of what we look like. But it's very difficult to have an image of our own act of looking or to have a true image of our own hands as they are moving. It's the Other who knows what our hands and eyes are like. These – how do you say – these gestures of the hands, are seen better by the Other than by myself.

And when you see this what do you think?

It's uncanny. It's bizarre.

But I don't have the desire to destroy it.

It's a very nice gift she's given me.

That she's given a small narcissist.

An old narcissist.

CLOSE UP: DERRIDA PORTRAIT

We Are…

INT. CATHEDRAL GALLERY - PARIS - DAY

Standing next to Derrida in the Chapelle St-Louis de la Salpetriere is the exhibit's artist, Dominique Renson. In the background hangs the portrait of Derrida. Off-screen, AZK asks DERRIDA:

AZK (O.S. re: Portrait**)**
And when you see this, what do you think?

DERRIDA
This portrait of me? It makes me very anxious. We've already spoken a great deal about the difficult rapport I have with my image. So I arrived here quite worried. But I'm not going to make any aesthetic evaluations. I can only say "I accept."

AZK (O.S.)
It's a strange feeling isn't it?

DERRIDA
It's very strange. But there are strange things against which one revolts, and others which one accepts. It's uncanny. It's bizarre. But I don't have the desire to destroy it as I often have with other photos or images. It's a very nice gift she has given me. That she's given to a little narcissist. (Pause) An old narcissist.

Laughter.

CUT TO: *We Are…*

INT. LA COUPOLE RESTAURAN - PARIS - NIGHT

CAMERA zooms in from a long shot to reveal DERRIDA in animated dinner conversation. As we watch from afar, we hear:

VOICEOVER
There is not narcissism and non-narcissism. There are narcissisms that are more or less comprehensive, generous, open, extended. What is called non-narcissism is in general but the economy of a much more welcoming and hospitable narcissism. One that is much more open to the experience of the Other as Other. I believe that without a movement of narcissistic reappropriation, the relation to the Other would be absolutely destroyed, it would be destroyed in advance. The relation to the Other, even if it remains asymmetrical, open, without possible reappropriation, must trace a movement of reappropriation in the image of one's self for love to be possible. Love is narcissistic. (POINTS 1992)
CAMERA slowly zooms out. Derrida's image recedes and then disappears amidst the throng of customers and waiters in the foreground. The zoom out continues until it is apparent that the camera has been shooting this entire sequence from outside the restaurant. The lights of passing cars reflect off the restaurant's large plate glass window.

Wait a second - cut.

One starts to reflect on one's response...

And the reflector interrupts the reflection.
Okay, repeat your question.

CUT TO: INT. RENE AND CHANTAL MAJOR'S LIVING ROOM - PARIS - NIGHT

Derrida is seated on the couch. His wife, MARGUERITE DERRIDA, a psychoanalyst, settles in beside him. The room is elegant and well appointed. Champagne glasses visible. A dinner party in progress.

Off-screen AZK attempts to interview the couple.

AZK (O.S.)
How did you two meet?

Marguerite laughs – when suddenly the film IMAGE drops out and power is abruptly cut.

AZK (O.S.)
Wait a second – cut.

The technical problem is quickly fixed. Image restored. But Derrida playfully takes advantage of this to deflect from the intimacy of the posed question.

DERRIDA
How can I start to think about responding to your question when you interrupt me to adjust the lights and then you interrupt me a second time – I can't do it.

AZK (O.S.)
So you never can forget the camera?

DERRIDA
But when I forget, there's a problem, and I'm forced to stop mid-sentence for you to readjust – what do you call that there… Protector?

CREW PERSON
Reflector.

MARGUERITE (almost simultaneous echo)
Reflector.

DERRIDA
Oh, reflector. One starts to reflect on one's response, and the reflector interrupts the reflection. It's difficult. Okay, repeat your question.

Laughter.

AZK (O.S.)
How did you two meet?

DERRIDA
Should we tell or no?

MARGUERITE
Go ahead tell. Tell.

How did you two meet?

I'm not going to tell you everything.

No. I'm just going to tell you superficial things.

I was a student with Marguerite's brother.

Do you remember the first time you saw Jacques?

DERRIDA

I'm not going to tell you everything. No. I'm just going to tell you superficial things. I was a student with Marguerite's brother at the same school – Ecole Normale Supérieure, 1952.

MARGUERITE

So there was a pretty strong probability that we'd meet.

DERRIDA

Then one winter, the first year we were together at this school, we went skiing together, her brother, me and some friends. And that's when I met Marguerite. I'm not going into more detail, but it was in '53. And then we didn't see each other for awhile, and then she invited me to have lunch with her family, and it started like that.

AZK (O.S.)

Marguerite, Do you remember the first time you saw Jacques?

CUT TO: INT. LIVING ROOM - LAGUNA BEACH - CALIFORNIA - DAY

Derrida is in front of a TV monitor, where, in a future time, he watches the interview with himself and Marguerite as it continues to unfold.

MARGUERITE (On Monitor)

Yes. Yes. In the snow.

DERRIDA (On Monitor)

She seems to be surprised that we actually remember…

MARGUERITE (On Monitor)

He came to the village in the mountains where I was staying.

BACK TO: INT. MAJOR'S LIVING ROOM - PARIS –NIGHT

Where original conversation took place. The interview continues.

DERRIDA

You've hit an area where you're not going to get much information from us. It's very difficult to speak of these things in front of a camera. I can give you the facts, the dates… We were married in the States in 1957. These are facts. Raw facts.

AZK (O.S.)

Yes. It seems you have rules – you've already decided to only tell me facts. Why have you imposed this decision to not disclose anything?

MARGUERITE

It's just not that easy…

CUT TO: INT. DERRIDA'S KITCHEN - MORNING

Derrida and Marguerite are caught in the midst of their morning routine. Derrida butters his toast, Marguerite sorting dishes. All in silent concert.

In the snow.

He came to the village in the mountains where I was staying.

She seems to be surprised that we actually remember...

It's very difficult to speak of these things in front of a camera.

I like that scene precisely because we don't say anything.

Finished, Marguerite gathers her things, prepares to leave. She bends over Derrida in kitchen and lightly kisses his head, then turning to CAMERA before exiting the front door:

MARGUERITE
Okay, goodbye everybody. Have fun.

CUT TO: INT. LIVING ROOM - LAGUNA BEACH - CALIFORNIA - DAY

Derrida has just completed watching on a television monitor the interview with Marguerite and himself at the Major's house. AZK sits beside Derrida on the couch.

AZK
What I'd like to ask you about now is this question of the anecdote. At the biography conference you quoted Heidegger as saying that one could sum up the life of Aristotle as: Aristotle was born, he thought, and he died. And then when I asked you about your relationship with Marguerite, you said, "I can give you the facts, the dates, and that's it." Can you offer some commentary on that?

DERRIDA
Even though I'm not in agreement with Heidegger when he says the life of a philosopher can be summed up as his birth, death, and thought, and I can explain the reasons why I'm not in agreement with him; Nevertheless, I feel close to him and understand what he says, and in a certain manner I subscribe to his belief as well. That is to say if the story of one's life, the details, the anecdotes, the daily events, can only be inadequately told, then what remains essential for both me and Heidegger to know, is what a person thinks and writes philosophically. When I said earlier in that clip you showed me that you're not going to get much information from us, it wasn't simply because I believed things had to be hidden, but because it's difficult to speak of personal things under these conditions, when one is only able to say a few phrases in front of a camera. Even when I confide things that are very secret, I don't confide them in mode of a story. At times, I provide certain signs, facts, dates, but otherwise, I don't write a narrative. And so the question for me is the question of narration, which has always been a serious question for me. I've always said I can't tell a story. I'd love to tell stories, but I don't know how to tell them. And I've always felt that the telling is somehow inadequate to the story I'd want to tell. So I've just given up telling stories. I've just given up.

CUT TO: INT. A LOS ANGELES STUDIO - DAY

DERRIDA WATCHING HIMSELF AS HE WATCHES HIMSELF WITH MARGUERITE AT THE MAJOR'S HOUSE – this time in a Los Angeles Studio. One more layer added to the mix, one more layer to buffer the account of their first encounter.

AZK (O.S.)
How did you two meet?

DERRIDA (on MONITOR)
Should we tell or not?

MARGUERITE (on MONITOR)
Go ahead tell.

DERRIDA (on MONITOR)
I'm not going to tell you everything. No. I'm just going to tell you superficial things.

BACK TO: INT. LIVING ROOM - LAGUNA BEACH - CALIFORNIA - DAY

AZK (O.S.)
Was it strange to see something you have no memory of?

DERRIDA:
Yes, I don't remember at all the first time you asked me and Marguerite about how we first met. I don't remember this at all. I like that scene precisely because we don't say anything. We think the same thing, but we don't say it. I was moved by this scene, I liked it a lot. But I liked it precisely because we said nothing. We were about to say something but we remained on the edge of an impossible confidence.

EXT. EHESS - PARIS - DAY

Derrida and Marguerite exit the University and walk out its gate and along the street. Through the iron fencing we see Marguerite's hand gently pat Jacques' back.

CUT TO: INT. STUDIO, LOVE IMPROVIZATION #2 - PARIS - DAY

Derrida is standing against an overexposed background, beside a large mirror. AZK is in the foreground, addressing Derrida.

AZK
Just whatever you want to say about love…

DERRIDA
About what?

AZK
Love.

DERRIDA
Love or Death?

AZK
Love, not death. We've heard enough about death.

DERRIDA
Love?

AZK
Love.

DERRIDA
I have nothing to say about love. At least pose a question. I can't examine "love"

Whatever you want to say about love...   *Love or death?*   *At least pose a question. I can't examine "love" just like that.*   *Matbe that's what you want me to say in front of the camera.*

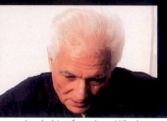

You can't ask this of me Amy. Why have philosophers always spoken of love?   *The heart of love is divided between the Who and the What.*   *What is it "to Be?" What is Being*

just like that. You need to pose a question. I'm not capable of talking in generalities about love. I'm not capable...Maybe that's what you want me to say in front of the camera, that I have nothing to say about love in general.

AZK

Could you explain why this topic has concerned philosophers for centuries? It's an important philosophical subject, isn't it?

DERRIDA

You can't ask this of me Amy. Why have philosophers always spoken of love? That's how philosophy started – No, no. It's not possible. I have an empty head on love in general. And as for the reason philosophy has often spoken of love, I either have nothing to say, or I'd just be reciting cliches.

AZK

Plato often spoke about this, maybe you could just talk about that.

DERRIDA

One of the first questions one could pose...I'm just searching a bit...is the question of the difference between the who and the what. Is love the love of someone or the love of some thing? Okay, supposing I loved someone. Do I love someone for the absolute singularity of who they are? I love you because you are you. Or do I love your qualities, your beauty, your intelligence? Does one love someone, or does one love something about someone? The difference between the who and the what at the heart of love, separates the heart. It is often said that love is the movement of the heart. Does my heart move because I love someone who is an absolute singularity, or because I love the way that someone is? Often love starts with some type of seduction. One is attracted because the other is like this or that. Inversely, love is disappointed and dies when one comes to realize the other person doesn't merit our love. The other person isn't like this or that. So at the death of love, it appears that one stops loving another not because of who they are, but because they are such and such. That is to say, the history of love, the heart of love, is divided between the who and the what. The question of Being, to return to philosophy – because the first question of philosophy is: What is it "to Be"? What is Being? The question of being is itself always already divided between the who and what. Is "Being" some one or some thing? I speak of it abstractly, but I think that whoever starts to love, is in love, or stops loving, is caught between this division of the who and the what. One wants to be true to someone – singularly, irreplaceably – and one perceives that this someone isn't x or y. They didn't have the qualities, properties, the images, that I thought I'd loved. So fidelity is threatened by this difference between the who and the what.

INT. DERRIDA'S KITCHEN - RIS-ORANGIS - DAY

He sorts through cutlery and converses with Amy off-screen.

DERRIDA
What did you think of my...

AZK (O.S.)
What did I think of your family? Very nice, very warm.

I love my sister very much. She is very sweet.

My sister is someone with whom I never,

throughout my entire life, fought over anything.

Except for when you tried to set her on fire in her crib?

DERRIDA
You thought they were nice?

AZK (O.S.)
Yes. Different from you.

DERRIDA
Yes, very different, and different from each other also. I love my sister very much.
She is very sweet. Her husband also.

AZK (O.S.)
They were very welcoming and hospitable…

DERRIDA
My sister is someone with whom I never, throughout my entire life, fought over
anything. There was never – between my sister and me – the least little… (in English)
How do you call this..?

AZK (O.S.)
Dispute?

DERRIDA
No, no, not even that… (there was) Absolute peace.

AZK (O.S.)
Except for when you tried to set her on fire in her crib?

DERRIDA (laughing)
That's the first and last time!... You remember this?....

We Return to:

INT. RENE & CHANTAL MAJOR'S LIVING ROOM - NIGHT

*General introductions and hellos. Champagne being poured. For the Derridas and
Majors, as well as the Film Crew.*

DERRIDA
The people who watch these images will think: "He's a fanatic of chips."
(He bites into a chip.)
"He drinks champagne in a magnificent home every day."

MARGUERITE (to Camera Crew)
If you'd like something, help yourself.

RENE
To everyone's good health…

He includes the Camera Crew in his toast.

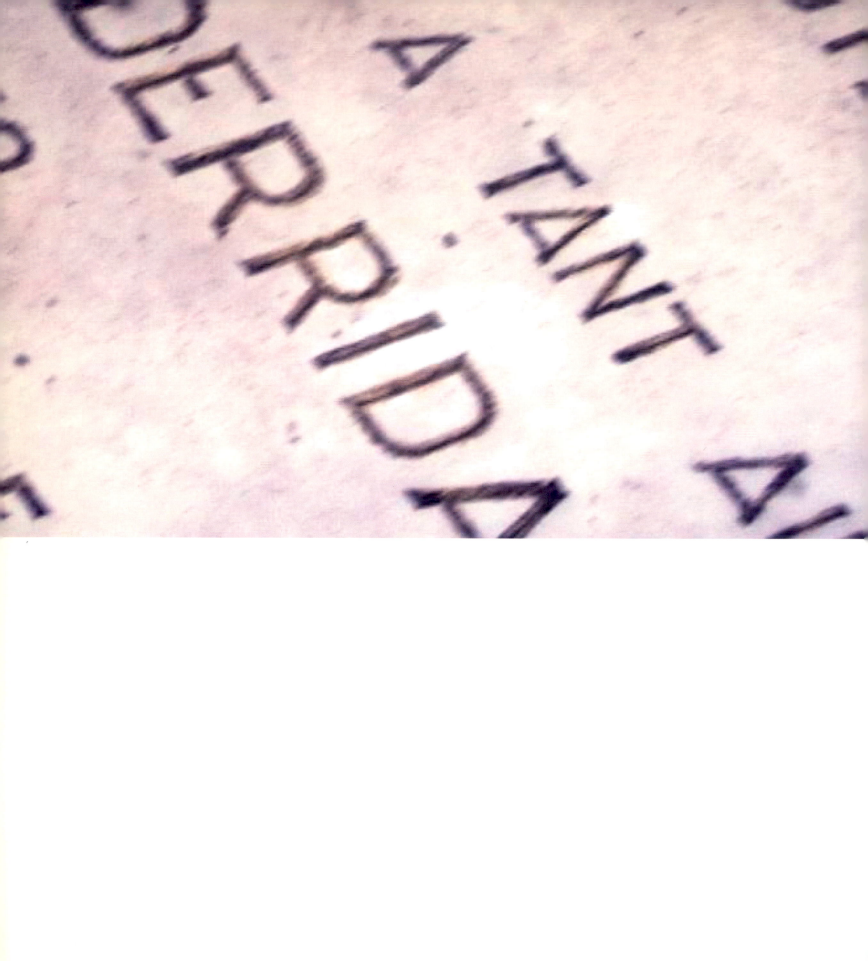

INT. RENE & CHANTAL MAJOR'S LIVING ROOM - PARIS - NIGHT - LATER

Derrida is sitting on a couch beside Rene Major.

DERRIDA
We were in the middle of comparing our two surgical operations.

RENE
You must understand, this is our way of getting him to talk about his body,

DERRIDA
I've written a lot about my mother's kidney stone. My mother, at 47, had been feeling sick, so they took an x-ray. And by chance they found a whole set of kidney stones. And so they operated to remove them, but found they couldn't remove them because one stone was so enormous that they were obliged to remove her whole kidney. So my mother lived with just one kidney from age 47 to 90. And she always kept in her house this spectacular stone.

Using fingers like a caliper, Derrida illustrates the immense size of his mother's KIDNEY STONE.

CUT TO: CEMETARY - NICE - DAY

Another stone. A JEWISH CEMETRY in Nice, France. Where Derrida's parents are buried. Hebrew lettering etched darkly in the rock. As we watch we hear AZK reading from Derrida's CIRCUMFESSION:

VOICEOVER
And I am writing here at the moment when my mother no longer recognizes me, and at which, though still capable of speaking or articulating, a little, she no longer calls me and for her and therefore for the rest of her life, I no longer have a name, that's what's happening, and when she nonetheless seems to reply to me, she is presumably replying to someone who happens to be me without her knowing it, if knowing means anything here, like the other day in Nice when I asked her if she was in pain ("yes") then where? It was February 5 1989, she had, in a rhetoric that could never have been hers, the audacity of this stroke about which she will alas, never know anything, no doubt knew nothing, and which, piercing the night replies to my question: "I have a pain in my mother", as though she were speaking for me, both in my direction and in my place.

CAMERA continues to wander through the graveyard, floating like a spirit across the fragmented tombstones.

VOICEOVER (CONT.)
I stop for a moment over a pang of remorse, in any case over the admission I owe the reader, in truth that I owe my mother herself for the reader will have understood that I am writing for my mother, perhaps even for a dead woman, for if I were here writing for my mother, it would be for a living mother who does not recognize her son, and I am paraphrasing here for whomever no longer recognizes me, unless it be so that one should no longer recognize me, another way of saying, another version, so that people think they finally recognize me… (CIRCUMFESSION 1992)

In Rwanda, the refugees are continuing their exodus.

There are now 45,000 who are walking towards Tanzania.

CAMERA hovers past MOTHER'S tombstone before levitating into the clear white sky.

INT. DERRIDA'S KITCHEN - RIS-ORANGIS - DAY
Derrida prepares lunch alone while listening to news on the radio.

RADIO (filtered)
The military chief of the Hezbollah, the pro-Iranian movement, was killed this morning in South Lebanon by an attack from an Israeli helicopter which destroyed the car of the Hezbollah chief. Israel then launched an operation targeting many positions of the Hezbollah in South Lebanon. In Rwanda, the refugees are continuing their exodus. There are now 45,000 who are walking towards Tanzania.

DERRIDA'S VOICE (O.S.)
The racism that I suffered from the most was the anti-Semitism that was permanent in Algeria…

We Are…

INT. LIVING ROOM, LAGUNA BEACH - CALIFORNIA - DAY

Derrida addressing off camera interviewer:

DERRIDA (CONT'D)
The racism that I suffered from the most was the anti-Semitism that was permanent in Algeria, and was even more greatly unleashed before the war. In 1940, when I was ten, anti-Semitism became the official doctrine of the French government. They expelled from school all the Jewish children, all the Jewish professors, and all the Jewish administrators, with just a few exceptions. So when I was ten, I was thrown out of school. My brother and sister as well. No one told us why. One day the principal just said, "Go home and your parents will explain." But what was most painful wasn't simply the administrative decision to expel us from school. It was what took place in the streets – the insults, the children calling us "dirty Jews." This violence that was continually expressed towards us. This was our daily experience. The persecution of children towards other children. It wasn't the adults. It was my classmates as they left school who picked on and insulted the "dirty Jews." Sometimes they beat us.

This very "rich" and painful experience naturally made me very sensitive to racism and anti-Semitism. I exercise an extreme vigilance against all acts of anti-Semitism, even when they are disguised or presented covertly. But the paradox of this situation, is that at the moment when I was expelled from school and the French Christian community, I wasn't happy to be enclosed in the Jewish community either. There was a Jewish school that my parents had enrolled me in. (With all the Jewish professors that had been fired, it was easy to reconstitute a really good school.) But I didn't like this school either. I was ill at ease. So there was at the same time a part of me that rejected solidarity with the Jewish community. These were the years that very much counted for me. I was very marked by this double experience of suffering both from anti-Semitism and my own discomfort within the Jewish community.

EXT. ROBBEN ISLAND - SOUTH AFRICA - DAY
Derrida arrives at ROBBEN ISLAND to visit President Mandela's prison cell.

This is the cell where President Mandela spent 18 years.

One must forgive what is unforgivable and so do the impossible.

WARDEN
This is cell where President Mandela spent 18 years.

DERRIDA
How much?

WARDEN
18 years. You will notice that in this cell there is no water facility or toilets.

As Derrida inspects the interior of Mandela's cell —
We Hear:

VOICEOVER
As soon as there is the One, there is murder, wounding, traumatism. The One guards against the Other, it protects itself from the Other. But in the movement of this jealous violence it compromises in itself its self-otherness or self difference. The difference from within one's self, which makes it One. The One as the Other. At one and the same time, but in a same time that is out of joint, the One forgets to remember itself to itself. It keeps and erases the archive of this injustice that it is, of this violence that it does. The One makes itself violence, it violates and does violence to itself. It becomes what it is, the very violence that it does to itself. The determination of the self as One is violence. (ARCHIVE FEVER 1995)

CARD: In August 1998, Derrida was invited to speak at several South African universities. He chose to address the topic of forgiveness.

EXT. ESTABLISHING SHOT OF CAPETOWN - SOUTH AFRICA - DAY
INT. UNIVERSITY OF THE WESTERN CAPE - SOUTH AFRICA - DAY

Derrida stands at a lectern before a large audience.

DERRIDA'S VOICE
More than once we will be faced with the effects of a preliminary question which is the question: who or what? Does one forgive someone for a wrong committed or does one forgive someone something? Someone who, in whatever way, can never totally be confused with the wrong doing or the moment of the past wrong doing nor with the past injury. So, the question is, who or what? Do we forgive someone or do we forgive someone something?

SOME TIME LATER MODERATOR
Ok, a final, final question. There is a very anxious question…

He selects a STUDENT sitting on her desk, eager to pose question.

STUDENT
So you're a white Western male, speaking to a white audience. We are part of the previous oppressive community in South Africa. And you are speaking to us about unconditional forgiveness…Now you might have meant that pure forgiveness thing with a lot of irony, and maybe that is something that is really impossible – pure forgiveness being really impossible, but we sit here as potential objects of forgiveness and we are, all of us, you included, in a sense guilty. Now…don't you

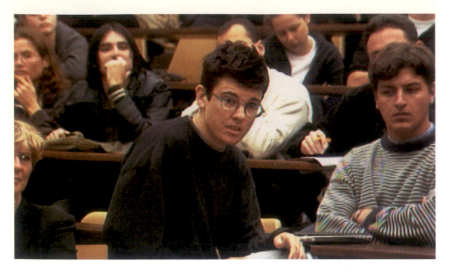

think it fills an ideological function speaking to us, telling us in a sense we should not repent, not ask for forgiveness, because then we "ruin" pure, unconditional forgiveness, while at the same time you are telling oppressed people they should forgive without expecting repentance.

DERRIDA

First of all, I take irony seriously; I take the problem of irony very seriously. And we need some irony that is something which challenges the common sensical concepts, and you can't do this without some irony. So there was no doubt some irony. Now of course in this context I understand your concern and I share your concern. I want to precisely draw a very rigorous border between the pure concept of forgiveness and the idea of reconciliation and the idea of excuse and the process which is going on. I think that as soon as you mix the concept of forgiveness with all the connected concepts which are at work in this current process, reconciliation, repentance, so on and so forth, then you first obscurely Christianize the process, you introduce confusion and obscurity in something which has to be as clear as possible.

EXT. LAGUNA BEACH - CALIFORNIA - DAY

Derrida continues to explicate his position.

DERRIDA

This gesture that I make when I talk of pure forgiveness, is a different gesture. I try to explain that any type of pure forgiveness is impossible. And that one can truly forgive only that which is unforgivable. If one forgives what is easily forgiven, one doesn't really forgive. One must forgive what is unforgivable, and so do the impossible. I also try and distinguish between reconciliation and forgiveness. A forgiveness that is demanded or accorded in order to achieve some type of reconciliation is not forgiveness. If I forgive solely to change a situation or to heal a wound, or if I forgive with a therapeutic intention or a psychoanalytic or ecological purpose or so that someone's health returns, or peace is restored, then to me, that is not pure forgiveness. That's a calculation. Now I might think it's a good calculation, one that must be made, but I wouldn't consider it pure forgiveness. I would regard it as something that is part of the process, a process of mourning, or reconciliation which is sometimes therapeutic, or politically necessary. And I approve of all these processes of reconciliation that are attempted in many parts of the world today. But since I am a philosopher who tries to be rigorous with what's said and tries to understand the meaning of words and evaluate their sense and implication, I refrain from calling these situations examples of pure forgiveness.

CUT TO: INT. TELEVISION STUDIO - SYDNEY - AUSTRALIA - DAY

An ABC FIELD PRODUCER gives the countdown for the beginning of another INTERVIEW.

FIELD PRODUCER

Five seconds to go. Five…four… three… two… one. In your own time.

INTERVIEW with ABC correspondent Andrea Stretton begins.

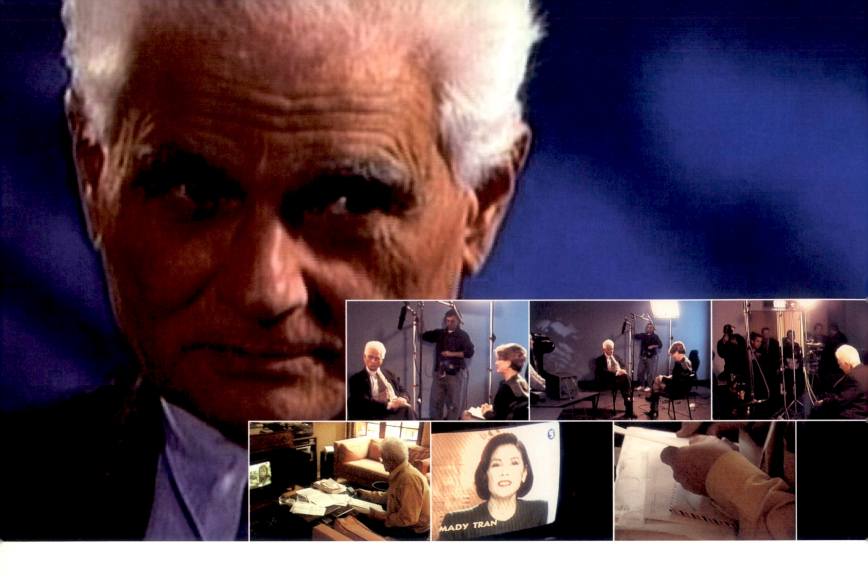

ABC NEWSCASTER
If I give you an example that I have often thought to myself that Seinfeld which is America's most popular ever sitcom, Seinfeld...

DERRIDA
What?

ABC NEWSCASTER
Sienfeld. Do you know the Seinfeld sitcom in America? If you think of a classic American, Jerry Seinfeld made this sitcom about a group of people living together, everything is about irony and parody and what you do with your kitchen cupboard is imbued with as much feeling or thought as whether someone believes in God, if you like, do you see anything in that?

DERRIDA (puzzled)
Deconstruction the way I understand it doesn't produce any sitcom, and if a sitcom is this and this, and the people who watch this and think that Deconstruction is this, the only advice I have to give them just is to read, stop watching sitcoms, and try and do your own homework and read.

CUT TO: *Derrida besieged – paparazzi style – by dozens of photographers snapping his picture as he obligingly poses.*

INT. DERRIDA'S HOME - RIS-ORANGIS - DAY

Derrida sitting in his den absently flicking the television channels as he sorts his mail. Over this We Hear:

VOICEOVER
It's not easy to improvise, it's the most difficult thing to do. Even when one improvises in front of a camera or microphone, one ventriloquizes or leaves another to speak in one's place the schemas and languages that are already there. There are already a great number of prescriptions that are prescribed in our memory and in our culture. All the names are already preprogrammed. It's already the names that inhibit our ability to ever really improvise.

ON TV: the face and name of a familiar news Broadcaster.

VOICEOVER (CONT'D)
One can't say what ever one wants, one is obliged more or less to reproduce the stereotypical discourse. And so I believe in improvisation and I fight for improvisation. But always with the belief that it's impossible.
The CAMERA seems to search the room, as if hunting for a subject, in a sense improvising itself.

VOICEOVER (CONT'D)
And there where there is improvisation I am not able to see myself. I am blind to myself. And it's what I will see, no, I won't see it. It's for others to see. The one who is improvised here, no I won't ever see him. (UNPUBLISHED INTERVIEW 1982)

There's a mirror. I'm speaking.
There's a camera.

You pose a question, I repeat it.

So I'm acting as both Narcissus and
Echo at one and the same time.

But Echo, in her loving and infinite
cleverness

arranges it is so that in repeating the
last syllables of the words of Narcissus

she appropriates his language and
makes it her own.

In repeating the language of another,
she signs her own love.

In repeating, she communicates
with him.

And as always with speech one is blind.

Now, how do two blind people love
each other?

That's the question...

INT. STUDIO - ECHO AND NARCISSUS IMPROVIZATION #3 - PARIS - DAY

In addition to several Cameras, Derrida is revealed here to be standing near an adjacent mirror. At times we are surprised to find the mirror's reflection to be Derrida – or vice versa – Derrida to be just a reflection. There is a constant play between the two

DERRIDA – IMPROV #3

I'll try now to answer your question about the story of Echo and Narcissus. If one focuses on the treatment of the image and not on the love story in the myth of Echo and Narcissus one sees the myth as about the relationship between specular image and voice between sight and voice between light and speech, between the reflection and the mirror. Speech is what's taking place here right now. There's a mirror. I'm speaking. There's a camera. You pose a question, I repeat it. So I'm acting as both Narcissus and Echo at one and the same time. And what's extraordinary in this scene, which I've examined in my seminars, is the moment when Echo traps Narcissus in a certain way. Echo, cursed by the jealous gods, was never allowed to speak for herself, and was only allowed to repeat the ends of other's phrases. But Echo, in her loving and infinite cleverness, arranges it so that in repeating the last syllables of the words of Narcissus, she speaks in such a way that her words become her own. In a certain way, she appropriates his language. In repeating the language of another, she signs her own love. In repeating she responds to him. In repeating, she communicates with him. She speaks in her own name by just repeating his words. And as always with speech, one is blind. To speak is to not see. So all speech to some extent is blind. And at base, Echo blindly but quite lucidly corresponds to Narcissus. It's a story of love, after all. She corresponds to Narcissus who is also blind, because Narcissus realizes that he can only see himself, that it's only his own image he is seeing in the water. To see only oneself is a form of blindness. One sees nothing else. And it's because of this that Narcissus cries. He cries, and in a way, he dies from not being able to see anyone else. Echo and Narcissus then are two blind people who love each other. Now how do two blind people love each other? That's the question.

DARKNESS….then LIGHT as Derrida finds the switch

We Are…

INT. DERRIDA'S HOME OFFICE - RIS-ORANGIS - NIGHT

Books everywhere, from floor to ceiling. Derrida offering a tour.

AZK
And what's this room?

DERRIDA
It's the new addition. I've only been working here a few months.

AZK
Did you read these?

Amy refers to two books by Anne Rice. Derrida pulls them out.

Did you read these?   *No, I never read these.*   *There was a time when I was teaching on vampirism, on cannibalism.*   *And someone gave them to me.*

You know, I haven't read all the books that are here.   *No?*   *No, only three or four.*   *But I read those four really, really well.*

DERRIDA

No, I never read these. There was a time I was teaching on vampirism, on cannibalism, eating the Other. So I made a number of references to vampires, and someone gave me these books. I don't even remember who gave them to me. No, I haven't read these. I haven't read all the books that are here.

AZK

But you've read most of them?

DERRIDA

No, No. Only three of four. But I read those four really, really well.

Laughter.

ANGLE ON: Adjacent Room

More books. But on a small cot by the door are diapers and baby paraphernalia.

DERRIDA

This was my son Pierre's bedroom. These things there are for when Vera, our grand daughter, comes to visit. She sleeps here.

AZK

That's nice.

DERRIDA

It's now another office, but it used to be Pierre's bedroom.

INT. LIVING ROOM - LAGUNA BEACH - CALIFORNIA - DAY

The room white and sunlit. Derrida is seated on a couch.

KIRBY DICK (O.S.)

If you had a choice what philosopher would you like to have been your mother?

DERRIDA (smiling, bemused, addressing Amy)
That's his style, that's his own style? (Pause) I have no ready answer for this, give me some time. My mother? Good question, it's a good question in fact. I'll try to tell you why its impossible for me to have any philosopher as a mother. My mother, my mother couldn't be a philosopher. A philosopher couldn't be my mother. That's a very important point. Because the figure of the philosopher is, for me, always a masculine figure. This is one of the reasons I undertook the deconstruction of philosophy. All the deconstruction of phallogocentrism is the deconstruction of what one calls philosophy which since its inception, has always been linked to a paternal figure. So, a philosopher is a Father, not a Mother. So the philosopher that would be my mother would be a post-deconstructive philosopher, that is, myself or my son. My mother as a philosopher would be my granddaughter, for example. An inheritor. A woman philosopher who would reaffirm the deconstruction. And consequently, would be a woman who thinks. Not a philosopher. I always distinguish thinking from philosophy. A thinking mother – it's what I both love and try to give birth to.

EXT. PARIS - DAY

Through a moving car window, we see a blighted urban landscape moving past in slow motion. As it passes, we hear:

VOICEOVER

That philosophy died yesterday, since Hegel or Marx, Nietzche, or Heidegger – and that philosophy should still wander toward the meaning of its death – or that it has always lived knowing itself to be dying; that philosophy died one day, within history, or that it has always fed on its own agony, on the violent way it opens history by opposing itself to nonphilosophy, which is its past and its concern, its death and wellspring;

More buildings and ongoing construction.

VOICEOVER (CONT'D)

… that beyond the death, or dying nature of philosophy, perhaps even because of it, thought still has a future, or even, as is said today, is still entirely to come because of what philosophy has held in store; or more strangely still, that the future itself has a future – all these are unanswerable questions. By right of birth, and for one time at least, these are problems put to philosophy as problems philosophy cannot resolve. (VIOLENCE AND METAPHYSICS 1964)

INT. NEW YORK CITY APARTMENT - DAY
CLOSE UP: AVITAL RONELL - NYU Professor, Friend

RONELL

Long ago I had dinner and his mother when she was alive was there and one of the great dictionaries in France had just come out and included differance with an "a" and that had happened that day and at dinner I said that we should have a party to celebrate the induction of difference with an "a" into the dictionary, this was a monumental encyclopedic event that ought to be marked and proper ceremony which I was very willing to arrange should take place, and Jacques' mother who was very ancient but noble, she said "Jackie did you spell difference with an A?" And she was mortified but it was so sweet, it was so fabulous and there was this moment where I also felt I had blabbed because, you know, now what's he supposed to do, explain to his mother? He doesn't – he's very modest, he doesn't talk about himself to his family.

CUT TO: DERRIDA'S BROTHER
INT. APARTMENT - NICE - FRANCE - EARLY EVENING

Derrida's brother, RENE, seated with his granddaughter on his lap.

RENE DERRIDA

Each time he gives us one of his books, or we attend one of his conferences we ask ourselves, "How does he do it?" How must his mind work to be able to come up with all these philosophical thoughts? Because we have brains as well, and we cannot come up with such things. Why him? Why is he able to come up with these philosophical thoughts and all these deductions and deconstructions?

We are not an intellectual family.

AZK (O.S.)
It's extraordinary.

CAMERAWOMAN (O.S.)
It's an enigma, isn't it?

RENE DERRIDA
Yes, it's a great enigma.

AZK (O.S.)
You don't see any links in your family?

RENE DERRIDA
Not at all, Not at all.

CAMERAWOMAN (O.S.)
It comes out of nowhere.

RENE DERRIDA
Out of nowhere.

AZK (O.S.)
And what would your parents say?

RENE DERRIDA
Well, my mother read a lot, but definitely not this sort of reading. We were not an intellectual family. Not at all.

CAMERAWOMAN (O.S.)
If you had to speculate where it came from...?

RENE DERRIDA
I would be incapable. Even if one searched past generations either on the side of my father or mother one couldn't find a link to Jackie's spirit.

CUT TO: *CARD: On April 17, 1995 a ceremony was held to commemorate the creation of a Derrida Archive in the United States at the University of California at Irvine.*

INT. LECTURE HALL - UNIVERSITY OF CALIFORNIA AT IRVINE - DAY

Faculty, students and Derrida at the inauguration of the UC Irvine's Derrida Archive.

DERRIDA
You can imagine how strange it is, not just to have someone gather your archive, but to attend the event of the inauguration of the archive. I realized the other day and this afternoon by looking at the archive in the library, with these black and gray urns accumulated like, of course, in a graveyard – we are always already mourning – Well, you know, among the concerns we have about where we are going to be buried, the question is – with whom...?

Audience laughter.

CUT TO: INT. DERRIDA ARCHIVE - UC IRVINE LIBRARY - DAY

Where EDDIE YEGHIAYAN, archivist, is offering a brief tour of Derrida's works.

YEGHIAYAN
This is the entire Derrida archive beginning there almost to the end, there's about 100 boxes.

We see Derrida pacing through the archive, as Eddie continues.

YEGHIAYAN (CONT'D)
He mentioned that his wife was kind of reluctant to see these materials go, that it was a kind of foretelling of his imminent death or something like that. And you know we then had the boxes still in our reading room – we were in a kind of different situation there – and he treated it like it was his little child. And I remember the manuscript was pushed out and he looked at it and touched the box, kind of sorry to see it go or be in another domicile or whatever.

CUT TO: INT. DERRIDA ARCHIVE - UC IRVINE LIBRARY - LATER - DAY

A student, alone, is looking over original editions of Derrida's books that are displayed in a glass case. One title prominently displayed is "Archive Fever".

CUT TO: CLOSE ON: MONITOR INT. - LOS ANGELES STUDIO - DAY

On the MONITOR we again see the image of Marguerite preparing to leave for the day. As Monitor revives this old image (this time in slow motion), We Hear:

VOICEOVER
The question of the archive is not a question of the past. It is not the question of a concept dealing with the past that might already be at our disposal. An archivable concept of the archive.

ON MONITOR – as before, Marguerite silently bends over Derrida, kisses his head and crosses to door.

VOICEOVER (CONT'D)
It is a question of the future, the question of the future itself, the question of a response, of a promise, and of a responsibility towards tomorrow.

CAMERA PULLS back to REVEAL Derrida watching the Monitor – where Maguerite has just exited. For a moment he's just watching a closed door.

VOICEOVER (CONT'D)
The archive – if we want to know what that will have meant, we will only know in times to come; not tomorrow, but in times to come. Later on, or perhaps never. (ARCHIVE FEVER 1995)

I would like to hear them speak about their sexual lives.

What is the sexual life of Hegel or Heidegger?

I'd love to hear about something they refuse to speak about.

Why do these philosophers present themselves asexually in their work?

There is nothing more important in their private life than love.

I'm not talking about making a porno film about Hegel or Heidegger.

I want them to speak about the part that love plays in their lives.

What are you going to do with all this?

We've been talking for two hours - no, 25 years we've been doing this film.

And you're going to edit this down to one hour...

You'll keep exactly what you think has to be kept. That will be your signatu[re]

OVER DERRIDA'S SHOULDER: the silent MONITOR.

> *On it plays a repetition of the identical footage seen earlier in the film, of himself and Marguerite sitting on the couch – both speaking and refusing to speak about*

how they first met.

CUT TO: INT. DERRIDA'S HOME - RIS-ORANGIS - NIGHT

> *Derrida seated in his livingroom*

AZK (O.S.)
If you were to watch a documentary about a philosopher – Heidegger, Kant or Hegel, what would you like to see in it?

Long pause. Then:

DERRIDA
Their sex lives. If you want a quick answer. I would like to hear them speak about their sexual lives. What is the sexual life of Hegel or Heidegger?

AZK (O.S.)
Why?

DERRIDA
You want a quick answer; you don't want justification of the answer. Because it's something they don't talk about. I'd love to hear about something they refuse to talk about. Why do philosophers present themselves asexually in their work? Why have they erased their private lives from their work? Or never talked about anything personal? There is nothing more important in one's private life than love. I'm not talking about making a porno film about Hegel or Heidegger. I want them to speak about the part that love plays in their lives. So you could take a microphone up to Hegel…One knows some things about Hegel or Heidegger already. But not from things they've said. I'd like to hear them speak on this.

AZK (O.S.)
And do you think you would want people to ask you such a question?

DERRIDA
Yes, I never said I'd respond to such a question but…in my texts there are already many things that reference this. I disguise things…but I don't do so in the same way as the other philosophers you've named. I've dissimulated of course, like everybody. But not in the same fashion. So to answer your question, I'd be very interested to hear other philosophers speak about this. That's not to say that I would tell you, even if you were to ask me. I speak when I want and when I can…and eventually, in the presence of my attorneys…

(Long pause.)
What are you going to do with all this? We've been talking for about two hours – no, 25 years we've been doing this film and you're going to edit this down to one hour. What are you going to keep? You will keep exactly what you think has to be kept. That will be your signature and your autobiography in a certain way.

EXT. LIVING ROOM - LAGUNA BEACH - CALIFORNIA - DAY

> *In slow motion, the camera creeps along the side of the house, almost as if it were stalking something.*

VOICEOVER
How can another see into me, into my most secret self, without my being able to see in there myself? And without my being able to see him in me.

> *CAMERA creeps along the exterior of the Laguna beach house hunting its mark.*

THROUGH A WINDOW – it finds DERRIDA seated inside, being interviewed and filmed by yet another camera.

VOICEOVER (CONT'D)
And if my secret self, that which can be revealed only to the other, to the wholly other, to God if you wish, is a secret that I will never reflect on, that I will never know or experience or possess as my own, then what sense is there in saying that it is "my" secret, or in saying more generally that a secret belongs, that it is proper to or belongs to some "one", or to some other who remains someone.

> *CAMERA moves to spy from another WINDOW – another look.*

VOICEOVER (CONT'D)
It's perhaps there that we find the secret of secrecy. Namely, that it is not a matter of knowing and that it is there for no-one. A secret doesn't belong, it can never be said to be at home or in its place. The question of the self: "who am I" not in the sense of "who am I" but rather "who is this 'I'" that can say "who"? What is the "I" and what becomes of responsibility once the identity of the "I" trembles in secret? (THE GIFT OF DEATH 1992)

INT. LIVING ROOM - LAGUNA BEACH, CALIFORNIA - DAY

> *A montage of shots of Derrida responding to questions.*

AZK (O.S.)
You asked me the other day if I regretted having undertaken this project and I was wondering if that was a projection if you've regretted it?

DERRIDA
No, so far no, perhaps one day I will regret this. So far, no.

CUT TO: **AZK (O.S.)**
Have you ever been in psychoanalysis yourself?

DERRIDA
No.

AZK (O.S.)
Would you ever consider it?

DERRIDA

No. I absolutely exclude this.

RESET: DERRIDA

AZK (O.S.)

Could you characterize any traumatic breaks in your own life?

DERRIDA

There have been, yes.

He pauses, as if about to reveal some further elaboration, then decides against it.

AZK (O.S.)

Thank you.

They both laugh at his reticence.

DERRIDA

Again, no I won't be able to, uh, no, no.
(Pause, again considering, then definitively:) No.

CUT TO: EXT. - PARIS STREET - DAY

From high above, DERRIDA AND CREW exit the building and walk down the street. We hear church bells tolling in the distance.

INT. LIVING ROOM - LAGUNA BEACH - DAY

Derrida sits in silence, waiting. Across his FACE a set of inscrutable expressions as crew members cut in and out in front and behind him setting up the upcoming interview shot. As we watch his impenetrable gaze we hear,

VOICEOVER

We will wonder what he may have kept of his unconditional right to secrecy, while at the same time burning with the desire to know, to make known, and to archive the very things he concealed forever. What did he conceal even beyond the intention to conceal? Beyond the intention to lie or to perjure. We will always wonder what, sharing with compassion in this archive fever, what may have burned of his secret passions, of his correspondences, or of his "life". Burned without him, without remains and without knowledge. Without the least symptom, and without even an ash. (ARCHIVE FEVER 1995)
Fade out on Derrida continuing to gaze absently outward, as he waits for the interview to begin.

END CREDITS

On October 23, 2002 DERRIDA opened theatrically at FILM FORUM in New York. That evening, Derrida and the filmmakers participated in a Q and A session with the audience. The following is a transcript of that discussion.

Q: I first want to make some comments. With all due respect to Sakamoto, there's a Charles Mingus riff that might have been a good postlude for this film. It's something that Mingus wrote when he was in Bellevue, which was called: "All the things I could be if Sigmund Freud's wife were my mother."

Also, in terms of the film's themes of genealogy, I'd like to ask Amy (the film's co-director), one question: On the website, why have you repressed information about your undergraduate education and the role of Andrew Parker and other professors at Amherst and at U Mass who introduced you to Derrida's writing….

Amy Ziering Kofman: Hey, Jenny Stone. I knew I recognized the voice!

Q: And my third question is about the archive and to Jacques Derrida: There's something really perturbing here about this posthumous filmic text. Most people have their archive constituted post mortem, as much as documentaries are ever even made about them. So, I guess my question would be: Are you in love or are you dead?

Jacques Derrida: Both. As you know I have this ambiguous feeling about archives. I'm happy that there are some archives already gathered; there's one in Irvine as well as one in Paris. But I have a very ambiguous relation to them both because, in a certain way, it's a bit (and this is something I say in the film) as if I were being asked to attend my own burial. But at the same time, I'm not simply unhappy even though my feelings are ambiguous. It's obvious that this film is, in itself, also an archive. And I was just talking about this a minute ago (outside with the filmmakers), that at the moment when I'm photographed or filmed, I can't help but have the intense feeling that such images will survive me; that as soon as I die, people will be even more interested and so, they will see these images. So I have this immanent relation to what's beyond my "lifetime", as you say in English. In fact, just this last spring, I was in the library at UC Irvine discussing with the librarian what is going to happen with this archive after – and I remember this English word because it's not easily translated into French – the archivist didn't say to me "after my death" – He said: "After your lifetime, what will happen?" "After your lifetime, what will happen if"… and so on. "After your lifetime…" So when I see the movie, I do think: What will happen after my lifetime? But for now, I am still here.

Q: This is perhaps not so much related to the film, but you talked a bit in the film about the "always already" in some texts and I wondered if you could talk about what contemporary works you think most invite, demand, or perhaps contain, a deconstructionist reading.

JD: I missed the last part of your...

Q: What contemporary works of the past couple of years do you think most demand a kind of deconstructionist reading?

JD: I see no exception – everything, every text. Do you mean philosophical or journalistic texts? Everything! Everything requires deconstruction. Not only texts in the narrow sense, but everything. Deconstruction is not something that you just apply. Deconstruction is already at work – "always already" as you say – always already at work within the thing to be deconstructed. When you deconstruct, you don't use a tool to deconstruct something. You find, in the thing itself – the text itself, if you want – something already self-deconstructing. And nothing can escape this, in terms of politics, philosophy, every day life. So I see no exceptions to this.

Q: You spoke a bit about Heidegger in the film. What about Sartre? Did you have a relationship with him, and what do you think of his work?

JD: What kind of relationship? (Laughter). No. Obviously, I've read him, ever since I was very young. And he was, when I was a young student, one of the major philosophers. But I never met him, if that's what you mean by your question. I read him intensely when I was young, and then I departed from him. I realized he was not a strong philosopher. Then I came back and now I'm more interested in him than I was, say, ten or twenty years ago. It's complicated. But it's still a question for me how this man, who is not a very powerful philosopher, not a very good writer, either; who made so many mistakes in politics – who made mistakes all the time – nevertheless, is still such an admired figure in France. In fact, he's one of the most popular figures in France; he's very popular. When he was buried, by the way, there were millions of people in the street, which is quite an achievement for a philosopher. (Laughter). So, that's my question. I have a lot of sympathy and respect for his sense of justice. Even if he was wrong and he missed many points in politics, the inspiration of his moves was generous and I appreciate that. But no... I don't owe him anything in philosophy, if that's what you mean, but I admire his generosity – I admire the ethical and political generosity of the man. But, no, I didn't mention him (in the film). Someone the other night also asked me, "Why didn't you mention Sartre (in this film)?" But there are so many other people that I also don't mention, French and non-French....

Q: I was curious as to why Amy chose to use her own voice in reading the texts in the film.

AZK: That decision was something Kirby and I struggled with for a long time. And every time we did test screenings in LA people people would say, "Get an actor, Amy; do yourself a favor." But we finally thought that it was most appropriate for us to use the voice of one of the filmmakers (as the voice reading the text quotations) in the film, since our film is very much about issues of translation and the type of Echo and Narcissus relationship to Jacques and his work that we, as filmmakers, have. So we decided that it would actually add another layer to the film if it was my voice reading the texts, as it would further call attention to the filmmaking process, and underline this filmmaker/subject relationship, as well as call attention to issues of interpretation, translation, appropriation – so it was a combination of all these different considerations. That's basically why we ended up doing it this way.

Kirby Dick: Right. We didn't want to completely efface the role of the filmmaker in the film, so that's why we chose to put Amy in as a character in the film; but we chose to use her only, for the most part, in the margins, which is why at times you see only her hair (within the frame), or she's shot from the back. But throughout the film, Jacques is responding to someone and I think it's important to have a reference to that act, as a part of the documentary process.

Q: I have a question for the filmmakers. I'd like you to comment on the existence of another film, "D'ailleurs Derrida" and how you related to this film. Was it something you worked against? Was it something that surprised you because it appeared as you were already working on your film? How do you see that relationship?

KD: Well, we had been working on our film for a number of years when this other film came out, which was a film that was made for ARTE (French television) and it was an hour long television program, I believe. And, at that time we had already established the direction of our film, so there wasn't anything that we actually could take from that film. And our film, I think, has a much broader attack. We're dealing with a wider range of issues, I would say, than that film, so, no, there wasn't really any type of influence.

 Of course we would welcome any and all films on Jacques. I think it's wonderful. There should be an even greater cinematic record of Jacques…

JD: There should be a film every year. (Audience laughter)

Q: I was just wondering: how did you get Mr. Sakamoto involved in the film?

AZK: Kirby and I were working with an editor at the time, Curtiss Clayton, who is a Hollywood editor and filmmaker, and we asked him for some suggestions of major composers that he thought would be appropriate for this film, and he came up with a list. And so I bought a bunch of CDs of these composers and reviewed their work. And I heard Sakamoto's work and played it for Kirby, and told him that I felt that it was the right match. But we had no connections or contacts to him. So I just went onto his website – it's sort of a funny story – and his website is totally fascinating; it completely seems to be on some level channeling Jacques' work. It's just these letters floating around and you have no idea what you're clicking on – absolutely no idea. You click on a letter and, say, a poem comes up.

So I'm sort of floundering around this website thinking, "Well, this is appropriate." But there was no way of reaching Ryuichi listed on the website at that time. There was no address, there was no management company, there was nothing but all these floating letters. But I saw that there was the name of the website designer, so I called the website designer who was in London at the time and I said, "Here's who I am, I want to reach Ryuichi, and here's what I'm doing." And he said, "Alright, I'll put in a call for you." I thought, "Well, that's that," but sure enough, they called and asked us to send them some footage. So we sent them some rough cuts and Ryuichi watched them and said, "Yeah, I'll do it." And I was like, "Oh God, now I have to tell him we have no money." Because by this time I'd done some research and he's like a million-plus a picture, so I called his manager, Evan Balmer, and said, "This is great and we'd love to work with you but we don't have money." And Evan said, "Yeah I kinda figured that out; you guys don't even have stationary." And then at that point, he said, "Did you know that Ryuichi has worked with Derrida's texts?" And he thought that we knew that, and that that was why we had approached him, but I didn't have any idea about any of that. (To Jacques:) Evidently, Ryuichi had written an opera a few years ago in which he'd used some excerpts from your work.

JD: I didn't know that.

AZK: Yeah, well, he owes you some money. (Laughter) But Ryuichi's participation really just came about through happenstance and caprice but lucky caprice, and we're very grateful.

Q: I'm just wondering why you agreed to participate in the film, what you expected from it, and what you thought of the result?

JD: Three different questions. First, as they can testify, I was against the film. I was really very, very reluctant at the beginning, very reluctant. And I said, "No, no." Then there was some misunderstanding and the "no" became "yes."

KD: A little translation problem.

JD: Then it took years and I was constantly – as the filmmakers can also testify – I was very nervous, really reluctant. Except for some moments when I just forgot there was some shooting going on. I had to accept the experience of knowing that this film would become an archive, and that it would, in fact, be signed by the filmmakers. That they would have a hundred hours of – how do you say this? – footage, from which they would keep only one and a half hours, and that ultimately this selection would of course be their selection; the film would be their work and I had no real initiative in it, no initiative. So I knew from the beginning that I would be exposed to their own autobiographical signature; that this would be their autobiography. And of course it was not a continuous shooting process – sometimes a year passed between shoots, and in the meantime I'd be quite busy with other things… teaching, traveling. This film was not my thing for six years.

And the last question is the most difficult. I love the film. What can I say? I know, given the amount of footage they have, another film would have been possible, perhaps a totally different film, perhaps a better one, I don't know, perhaps worse. My feeling is that it's done; it's done, it's irreversible. And I'm happy that it's been done, okay? Let me put it that way because I don't want simply to make compliments and to say, "I love the film." If I were here to say, "I love the film," I would be ridiculous, because it's me, okay? I won't say I love the film. Narcissism is one of the subjects of the film, so "Narcissus Loves the Film" would then appear as a headline on a review of the film.

No, the only thing I can say is that I was very anxious about it, during the years and years (it took to complete), and that I have been reassured, let's say, to a large extent, by what I saw. Let me put it that way.

Q: I was wondering: did you have any control over the editorial process, or did you give the filmmakers complete editorial control? And if so, did you ask them to take anything out of the film that was in any of the rough cuts, and if so, what was it (that you asked them to remove)?

JD: Not that I remember. Of course, there was a contract. Written or not written – there was a contract between us. It stated that I would give the authorization (for the film's release) only after I had seen the completed film; which meant that I wouldn't participate at all in the editing. Not at all. But I wouldn't let the film become public before I reviewed it, that was part of the contract. And I never asked for anything except one thing, I remember. I never asked for anything, any change, anything to be removed. I did not intervene at all, except – if I remember correctly – once I told Amy that Marguerite is shown too often in the kitchen. My wife is a psychoanalyst, she's not… I'm more at home than she is, so the image of Marguerite all the time in the kitchen would have been misleading and untrue and unfair, so I asked Amy to just change something about this. That's the only intervention that I made that I can remember. Is that true?

AZK: The yogurt.

JD: Hm?

AZK: The yogurt.

JD: The yogurt?

KD: There was a scene with you eating yogurt.

JD: Ah, the yogurt! Ah, I forgot. Of course. Of course, I had problems with my breakfast and I asked you to remove the famous yogurt scene out of the film. I just forgot.

AZK: That's for the DVD. (Laughter)

Q: What kind of music do you listen to, and why do you listen to it?

JD: No, no, no, no – I usually don't answer such questions. What would that mean? I love jazz and Bach and Mozart. You shouldn't ask such a question. I love music but I'm not an expert or anything. I have no real musical expertise, in the professional sense, but I love music and I listen to music all the time. And well, free jazz or Bach or Mozart.

Speaking of free jazz, once in Paris I appeared in public with Ornette Coleman. He asked me to come to one of his performances. We met in a hotel. There was a big discussion and he told me he was interested in my texts, so we met. Then he invited me to come to one of his concerts and to say anything I wanted and he would accompany me, improvising. So, I was quite scared. It was almost the same story (as with this film): Finally, I said yes. Although against it, I said yes. So I prepared a text, and Ornette Coleman started the concert and, as we agreed upon, at some point he called me onstage. And once onstage, I started reciting this special text that I'd written for this occasion as he accompanied me, improvising. But his fans were so unhappy with this strange man coming onstage with a written text that they started, uh, whistling? Sorry…

KD: Catcalling? Booing?

JD: So it was a very painful experience. But finally it turned into a happy event because the day after, in the newspapers, everyone mentioned this as something interesting. But, in fact, it was a painful experience for me.

So, I love Ornette Coleman – he's a good friend of mine – and that's the kind of music I like, among others.

Q: I have a question about the editing process. This film is very beautiful, very lyrical; there are very specific things you've chosen for us to know about Mr. Derrida and his philosophy. I'm wondering how long the editing process was, and how much you sort of knew about the form the film would take going into it, and how much of it evolved over the period of time that you were working on it?

KD: Well, it definitely evolved. One of the reasons that we both chose to undertake the film was the challenge it presented – in some ways the seeming impossibility – of working with Derrida's thought in a cinematic form. Obviously, the way to do this is not something that suggests itself immediately. One of the beauties of making documentaries is that they afford you lots of opportunities to rewrite and rewrite. Actually, the film's final form, which I think at this point I would describe as episodic – relying a great deal on the use of excerpts from his work – was only realized toward the very end of the film.

AZK: The only little short thing I'd add to that is that it was very much the situation that we would shoot, then edit, shoot, then edit. So each (post) production step always informed the next. So maybe Jacques wouldn't know why we were showing up again, but that next shoot was always informed by what we discovered in the editing process or what new attack we were trying to take. But what was interesting or challenging about the film is that there was no model. You know, you couldn't say: "Oh, let's see what they did with Freud", or "Nietzsche's got a great little film made about him… Let's have a look at that." So it took a long time to figure out the form; the challenge for us was, how do you deal with abstract and complex texts and still produce a rich, powerful visual experience?

Q: What is your opinion, Mr. Derrida, of Guy Debord and le Situationiste Internationale and the Internationale Lettriste?

JD: Let me ask you a question: what is the relationship between this question and the film? There is probably a relationship, but tell me what you have in mind by asking such a question now, because there are so many other possible questions – why this question, now?

Q: Well, just because I like Guy Debord, and there seems to be a connection, so I was wondering if for you there was this connection as well?

JD: Okay, well yes. I'm very interested in Guy Debord's work. I feel, in many ways, very close to what he did, more and more, I would say. And everything I say about the media, technology, the spectacle, and the 'criticism of the show', so to speak, and the markets – the becoming-a-spectacle of everything, and the exploitation of the spectacle. I think this (relationship) appears sometimes in the film, or at least (it appears) in what I write. So if there is a relationship between the film and my texts (in this way), then Guy Debord – in a way – will be…

Q: Honored.

JD: That's all I can say now. But I think you probably know that his work is read now more than when he was alive. At least that's the case in France. I don't know if he's read in the States, but in France he's read as presenting a precise critique and political analysis of the media, of the becoming-spectacle, the exploitation of the 'show' in politics and in the media, and television.
What's interesting is that in France people, especially the writers or the intellectuals who are often asked to appear on TV – sometimes almost every day – they [reflexively] mention Guy Debord as their master, and I hate this! So I never quote Debord when I'm on TV, and I'm almost never on TV – so I guess that's how, in my way, I'm true to Debord.

Q: For Monsieur Derrida: how do you feel about the term 'deconstruction' being so bandied about within the fashion world. Does it amuse you and/or irritate you to hear it used by people who probably don't know what it means?

JD: Well, I have – how do you say – "mixed feelings." On the one hand, I'm happy that the word circulates. And I try to understand why – despite the fact that people don't understand what it means or haven't even read, in fact, the texts they should have read (in order to understand what it means) – this term has become so popular. There is probably a reason why it's become fashionable in a number of fields, not only in the fashion world, but in many other fields as well. So there must be some thing, some reason, some serious reason why it's become fashionable. And I try to understand this. Even if people don't know what 'deconstruction' should really mean – seriously, philosophically – they understand something about deconstruction, and that's not meaningless. So finally I guess I'm amused, a little anxious, but, nonetheless quite interested. And finally, not unhappy.

KRISTINE MCKENNA / JACQUES DERRIDA – LA WEEKLY NOV 2002

Kristine McKenna: Can you recall the moment when you first realized that god, as the word is conventionally understood, was a notion you could never embrace?

Jacques Derrida: To discuss this we must insist on that definition of god – as the word is conventionally understood. But yes, I can recall it. While I was growing up I was regularly taken to a synagogue in Algiers, and there were aspects of Judaism I loved – the music, for instance. Nonetheless, I started resisting religion as a young adolescent, not in the name of atheism or anything negative, but because I thought the way religion was practiced within my own family was fraught with misunderstanding. I was shocked by the meaningless way my family observed religious rituals – I found it thoughtless, just blind repetitions. And there was one thing in particular I found and still find unacceptable, and that was the way honors were dispersed. The privilege of holding, carrying and reading the Torah was auctioned off in the synagogue, and I found that terrible. Then when I was thirteen, I read [Friedrich] Nietzsche for the first time, and though of course I didn't understand him completely, he made a big impression on me. The diary I kept then was filled with quotations from Nietzsche and [Jean Jacques] Rousseau, who was my other god at the time. Nietzsche objected violently to Rousseau, but I loved them both and wondered, how can I reconcile them both in me? I've never been able to, of course, but they're still both very present in my work and teaching. I never left them.

KM: In an interview he gave shortly after World War II but ordered withheld from publication until after his death in 1976, Heidegger said "philosophy after Nietzsche could offer neither help nor hope for mankind's future. All we can do is wait for a god to reappear. Only a god can save us now." Do you agree?

JD: I wouldn't use the term 'a god,' of course, but what's interesting to me in this statement is that Heidegger was anti-religious. He was raised a Catholic but he vehemently rejected Christianity, so the god he refers to is not the Jewish, Muslim, or Christian god we know. He refers to a god who not only hasn't come yet, but perhaps doesn't exist. He gives the name of god to the one who is hoped for, and implies that the one who'd come and save us will have the name of god. Of course I don't agree with this if it encourages hope for salvation, but if the statement means that we're waiting for the arrival of an unpredictable one, and that we must be hospitable to the coming of this one, then I've got no objection. This is a form of what I'd describe as messianicity without messianism, and we are by nature messianic. We cannot not be, because we exist in a state of expecting something to happen, awaiting the arrival of someone whom we hadn't anticipated.

KM: Do we set ourselves up for unhappiness living that way? There are many lives in which the arrival never occurs.

JD: Even if we're in a state of hopelessness and despair, a sense of expectation is an integral part of our relationship to time. Hopelessness is possible only because we do hope that some good, loving someone could come, and that's undeniable. If that's what Heidegger meant then I agree with him.

KM: Did you fear for your life as a child growing up during the second World War?

JD: No. My experience during the war was difficult, but it couldn't be compared with what happened to the Jews in Europe. There was terrible anti-Semitism in Algeria and all the Jews there were expelled from school, but there were no Germans in the country, no concentration camps, no massive deportation of Jews. But the traumas occurred nonetheless. When you are expelled from school without understanding why, it marks you.

KM: In Ron Rosenbaum's book of 1998, Explaining Hitler, he suggests that meaning itself was Hitler's final and ultimate victim, because coherent meaning simply cannot be found in the Holocaust. Do you agree?

JD: I'll go very slowly here. I know there are philosophers, some of whom are my friends, who think that what was absolutely new in the genocide of the Holocaust was that it had no sacrificial structure. It was cold, rational, industrial, and it was given no sacrificial meaning. I'm not sure that's true. I'm not prepared to answer that question without giving it a good deal more thought.

KM: What are the central questions philosophy came into existence to answer?

JD: First of all, how to handle one's life and live well together – which is also politics. This is what was addressed in Greek philosophy, and from the beginning philosophy and politics were deeply intertwined. We are living beings who believe we have the capacity to change life, and we place ourselves above other animals. I'm critical of the question of the animal and how it's treated in philosophy, by the way, but that's another issue. Still, we think we're not animals, and that we have the ability to make decisions and organize our lives. Philosophy poses the question: what should we do to have the best possible lives? I'm afraid we haven't made much progress in arriving at an answer to this question.

KM: In philosopher Peter Singer's controversial book of 1975, Animal Liberation, he made the case that animals and humans should exist on an equal moral plane: Do you agree?

JD: I'm very much in favor of a massive change in our relationship with animals, but I don't believe in what's referred to as the rights of the animal. This concept of rights has its roots in the philosophy of [Rene] Descartes, which is precisely responsible for the repression of the animal. So while I'm full of sympathy for the plight of the animal, I wouldn't subscribe to a charter outlining the rights of the animal.

KM: Are you a vegetarian?

JD: I'm not a strict vegetarian, but I'm more and more inclined not to eat meat.

KM: One could make the case that philosophy and theology are much alike in that both are systems of thought that have what could be described as tenuous ties to the physical world. What's the most significant difference between the two?

JD: This is a huge problem. I used to think – and this is rather Heideggerian, and though I don't always agree with Heidegger, in this respect I do – that philosophy cannot be disassociated from ontology and theology. That's why Heidegger coined the expression ontotheology. This refers to the area where the ontological question of being merges with the theological question of the most important being. It's very difficult to separate these two strands of thought.

KM: What's the difference between knowledge and wisdom?

JD: They aren't heterogeneous, and you can know lots of things and have no wisdom at all. Between knowledge and action there is an abyss, but the fact that there is an abyss shouldn't prevent us from trying to know as much as possible before making a decision. Philosophy is the love of wisdom. Philia is love and sophia is wisdom – that's the way it defined itself at the beginning, so the duty to be wise is what philosophy is. Nonetheless, decisions don't depend exclusively on knowledge. I try to know as much as possible before making a decision, but I accept the fact that at the moment of the decision I'll make a leap beyond knowledge.

KM: In a piece on Sir Karl Popper published in The New Yorker, Adam Gopnik commented that "Popper believed that competing hypotheses fought each other off nobly while we watched; the reality is that competing hypotheses are mauled, and then one creeps away to die in peace. No one ever really changes his mind about anything; there are just more minds that think the new way. Behaviorism, Freudianism – no one refuted them, really. They just passed away out of loneliness." Do you agree?

JD: No, I don't agree with that idea. I met Karl Popper in Sicily one year when we both received the Nietzsche Prize, and he made very little impression on me.

KM: Did arriving at the set of understandings that you presented in your three books of 1967 enhance the quality of your life and bring you greater happiness?

JD: I wouldn't say it made me happier, but it gave me the strength and motivation to continue. I lead a very active, exhausting life, and I'm sure I derive much of the energy required to maintain this schedule from the reception my work is given. People are generous with me and my work, and I'm sure I would collapse without that generosity. If someone had told me when I was twenty that I'd be doing what I do now at the age of 72, I wouldn't have believed it. I was more physically fragile then and I would've collapsed from doing a fraction of what I do now. The reception of the work gives me this energy.

KM: Why aren't there any female philosophers?

JD: Because the philosophical discourse is organized in a manner that marginalizes, suppresses and silences women, children, animals, and slaves. This is the structure – it's a fact, it would be stupid and unfair to deny it, and consequently there have been no great women philosophers. There have been great women thinkers, but philosophy is one very particular mode of thinking among other modes of thinking. But we're in a historical phase when things like this are changing.

KM: Would you describe yourself as a feminist?

JD: This is a huge problem, but in a certain way, yes. Much of my work has dealt with the deconstruction of phallocentrism, and if I may say this myself, I'm one of the first to put this question at the center of the philosophical discourse. Of course I'm in favor of ending the repression of women, particularly as it's perpetuated in the philosophical groundings of phallocentrism, so in that regard I'm an ally of feminine culture. But that doesn't prevent me from having reservations about some manifestations of feminism. To simply invert the hierarchy, or for women to appropriate the most negative aspects of what's conventionally viewed as masculine behavior benefits no one.

KM: What's the most widely held misconception about you and your work?

JD: That I'm a skeptical nihilist who doesn't believe in anything, who thinks nothing has meaning, and text has no meaning. That's stupid and utterly wrong, and only the people who haven't read me say this. This misreading of my work began 35 years ago and it's very difficult to destroy. I never said everything is linguistic and we're enclosed in language. In fact, I say the opposite, and the deconstruction of logo-centrism was conceived to dismantle precisely this philosophy for which everything is language. Anyone who reads my work with attention understands that I insist on affirmation and faith, and that I'm full of respect for the texts I read.

KM: Your book of 1997, Cosmopolitanism and Forgiveness, makes the point that forgiveness that seeks any kind of response is not forgiveness at all, but is in fact a negotiation. This idea is very Buddhist in nature, as is the rejection of dualistic thinking that runs through your work. You've often made the point that life can't be reduced to either/or dichotomies, but rather, life is the vast, immeasurable territory that stretches between two opposing positions. Are you aware of the parallels your work has with Eastern philosophy?

JD: Many people have commented on the relationship between my work and Buddhism, and Zen Buddhism in particular, but I must confess to having only a superficial knowledge of Buddhism. If Buddhism is a way of transcending binary oppositions, I would say yes.

KM: With sufficient understanding of the Other, could the impulse to kill be erased?

JD: The drive to kill will never be erased because it's part of the human animal. The human animal has a capacity for cruelty, and to make the Other suffer can be a source of pleasure. That isn't eradicable, but it doesn't mean we have the right to kill – and, one of the crucial functions of philosophy and thinking is to learn to handle and negotiate this irreducible drive. Cruelty is always there and we must do our best to control it and transform it into something good – and it can be transformed into things that are beautiful and sublime. When I write and teach there's an element of aggression in these activities, but I attempt to transform that aggression into something useful. Aggressive energy can be transformed into something more interesting than killing, and of course, you can kill without killing. I can kill the Other without putting an end to his or her life, and can be aggressive in a way that's not despicable.

KM: Concepts of territory and ownership seem to be at the root of much human conflict; where did these ideas originate, and why do we cling to them?

JD: These concepts have become quite destructive and while they needn't be abolished, they must be changed dramatically. The need for that change was central to politics throughout the 20th century. For many centuries the city was a crucially important center of activity and commerce, but with new technology that's no longer the case, and the politics of owning a place are different. Nevertheless, the place remains important. A friend of mine recently said there are two things today that can't be de-territorialized or virtualized: they are Jerusalem – nobody wants virtual Jerusalem, they want to own the actual soil

—and the other thing is oil. The capitalistic nation states live on oil, and although that could be changed, the whole society would collapse if it did. That's why oil is a problem. It's more of a problem in America than it is in Europe, but we share the same concerns. Everything is always more in America, for obvious reasons.

KM: What's the most significant historical event that's occurred over the course of your life?

JD: Because it's relatively fresh in the collective memory, many people would probably say nothing comparable to September 11th has happened for centuries, but I wouldn't agree. This isn't to diminish the significance of that event. I was in New York just after it happened and was deeply wounded by it. I'm in love with New York, and although I never found the Twin Towers beautiful, I had a senti-mental attachment to them and I'd taken many friends there over the years. I was staying in an apartment ten minutes from the site a few weeks after the attack occurred, and it took me a week before I had the courage to go there. Then, when I finally did go, my reaction was emotional beyond any political considera-tion. Since then, I've felt compelled to acknowledge this event every time I've spoken publicly. I can't avoid opening my lecture with a reference to it, and I'm very interested in how people perceive it, and why it's viewed as a monumental event. Is it a major event? I'm not sure what the answer is.

KM: You've been with the same woman for fifty years; to what do you attrib-ute the strength and longevity of your marriage?

JD: Is it so exceptional? Neither my wife or I have any special skills for marriage. What we have is love, so it's thanks to that, and to our children. For a long time I was against family, and I lived for several years with the person who became my wife with no intention of marrying. It took quite a while for me to accept the notion of marriage.

KM: Why does love die for many people?

JD: Love doesn't die, rather, it becomes buried by other things. Sometimes it's buried alive, or it's buried by another love. There are periods when a love can be shared and be inscribed into a life, then that period ends. People take divergent paths and the love must then remain secret. It's buried, but not forgotten. I never stop loving the people I love. We're not speaking of sexual love here, but when I love someone, it may happen that I stop declaring it or making it manifest, but I'm faithful to love. I cannot not be faithful to love because I have a passion for memory and faithfulness.

KM: Is the past more apt to be a source of pain or pleasure for people?

JD: This differs from one person to the next, but I'm fortunate in that I have a happy relationship with the past. I even keep happy memories of difficult parts of my life that I know were terrible. I'd like to repeat my life, and would accept that everything be repeated endlessly, exactly as it happened. The eternal return.

KM: How did becoming a father change you?

JD: I wouldn't say it changed me, but it's been a major event in my life. My two sons are the most important thing in my life, not only because I love them, but because both of them are extraordinary, exceptionally intelligent people. I'm intimidated by them and I'm always shy and anxious about their judgment. Both of them are philosophers, and they write – one is a poet who makes film. Their judgment counts for me more than anyone else's.

KM: In 1997 you gave the filmmakers Amy Ziering Kofman and Kirby Dick permission to follow you around and film you for the documentary, Derrida, which was released in 2002. Why did you agree to be filmed?

JD: I didn't do it out of a narcissistic desire, nor did I immediately agree to it. In fact, when Amy initially contacted me about doing the film I sent her a postcard telling her no, this won't be possible, but because my handwriting is impossible to decipher she misinterpreted the postcard as my saying yes! She finally did convince me, but I proceeded with deep reservations that had to do with the discomfort I've always felt about my image in photographs. I succeeded in publishing for almost twenty years without a single image of myself appearing in connection with my books, and there were two reasons for that. First, I had what you might describe as ideological objections to the conventional author photograph – a head shot, or a picture of the writer at his desk – because it struck me as a concession to selling and to media. The second reason was that I've always had a difficult relationship with my own body and image. It's hard for me to look at myself in photographs, so for twenty years I gave myself permission to erase my image on political grounds. Over the last decade, that became increasingly difficult because I was constantly appearing in public spaces at conferences attended by journalists, many of whom took pictures. It finally became impossible to control, and as I felt it was time to overcome this resistance I finally let it go.

KM: Why are you uncomfortable with your image? You're often described as being quite handsome.

JD: I'm happy to hear that, but it's not the relationship I have with my own image. I saw the film on the big screen the other day and there were moments that were terrible and I was horrified when I saw myself. I don't know if this warrants being printed, but when I'm filmed in profile it's more or less O.K., however, some of the frontal shots of my face are ghastly. Nonetheless, I was pleasantly surprised by how successfully the film intertwines the private everyday life of family, with things less private – a trip I took to South Africa during the filming, for instance – and reflections on big subjects. The film has a consistent through line in that it continually questions the biography of authors. Should a philosopher have a biography?

KM: How could a philosopher not have a biography?

JD: Of course he has a biography, but the question I raise is whether we should publish it. Should he himself narrate his own biography? Should he let his own life be public and be interpreted?

KM: How can you separate a philosopher's writing from his life?

JD: I don't know if you can, but most classical philosophers did try to separate them, and some of them succeeded. If you read philosophical texts of the tradition, you'll notice they almost never said "I," and didn't speak in the first person. Philosophy is something empirical and outside, something else.

KM: You don't think the philosophy is shaped by the life?

JD: It is, but the private empirical life is considered an accident that isn't necessarily or essentially linked to the philosophical activity or system. From Aristotle to Heidegger, they try to consider their own lives as something marginal or accidental. What was essential was their teaching and their thinking.

KM: There's a scene in the film in which you're asked, if you could hear the philosophers who've been important to you talk about anything, what you'd like to hear them talk about. You reply, "their sexual lives, because it's the thing they don't talk about," but when the interviewer then asks you about your own sexual life, you decline to answer. Why is this territory off limits?

JD: I declined to answer not because I think these things must be hidden, but because I don't want to disclose the most personal aspects of my life while improvising in front of a camera in a foreign language. If I'm to discuss such things I prefer to sharpen my own tools – my writing. If you read me you'll find there are many texts where I address these questions in my way. I don't want to disclose everything, but I don't hide, and certain texts – The Post Card: From Socrates to Freud and Beyond, [published in 1980], Glas [1974] – are autobiographical. My own life, my desires and loves are inscribed in all of my writing –in a certain way, of course. They're not confessions, but I do take the risk of making my life part of what I write.

KM: What's important to you today?

JD: How can I answer such a question? Many things private, public and political are important to me. Today I'm concerned with what's happening in the Middle East and in France. As you probably know, the far right candidate Jean-Marie Le Pen came in second in the first round of the French presidential elections on April 21st, and this reveals something in my country that disturbs me deeply. But I think of all these things with a constant awareness that I'm aging, I'm going to die, and life is short. I'm constantly attentive to the time left to me, and although I've been inclined this way since I was young, it becomes more serious when you reach 72.

KM: Have you made your peace with the inevitability of death?

JD: So far I haven't and I doubt I ever will, and this awareness permeates everything I think. It's terrible what's going on in the world and all these things are on my mind, but they exist alongside this terror of my own death. And it's not just death – one struggles with aging as well, because it forces you to make decisions about the future. Yesterday I had lunch with the librarian at Irvine, then I had dinner with the dean, so we could discuss the future. I left my archive here, so during this lunch we had to consider events referred to as "beyond my lifetime," in terms of my papers. And with the dean, I plan to return next year, but the following year I'll be 74, and it would probably be wise to reduce my schedule at that point. These decisions must be made now.

KM: At what point did you become an adult?

JD: This is an intriguing question. I've always believed everyone has more than one age, and I carry three ages within myself. When I was twenty I felt old and wise and full of experience, but now I feel like a child. There's an element of melancholy to this, because although I feel young in my heart, I know objectively that I'm not young. The second age I carry is my real age of 72, and everyday I'm confronted with signs that remind me of it. The third age I carry – and this is something I only feel in France – is the age I was when I began to publish, which for me was 35. It's as if I stopped at the age of 35 in the academy and the cultural world where I work. Of course that's not true, because in many circles I'm considered an old, well known professor who's published a lot. Nonetheless, I feel as though I'm a young writer who just started publishing, and people are saying "well, he's promising."

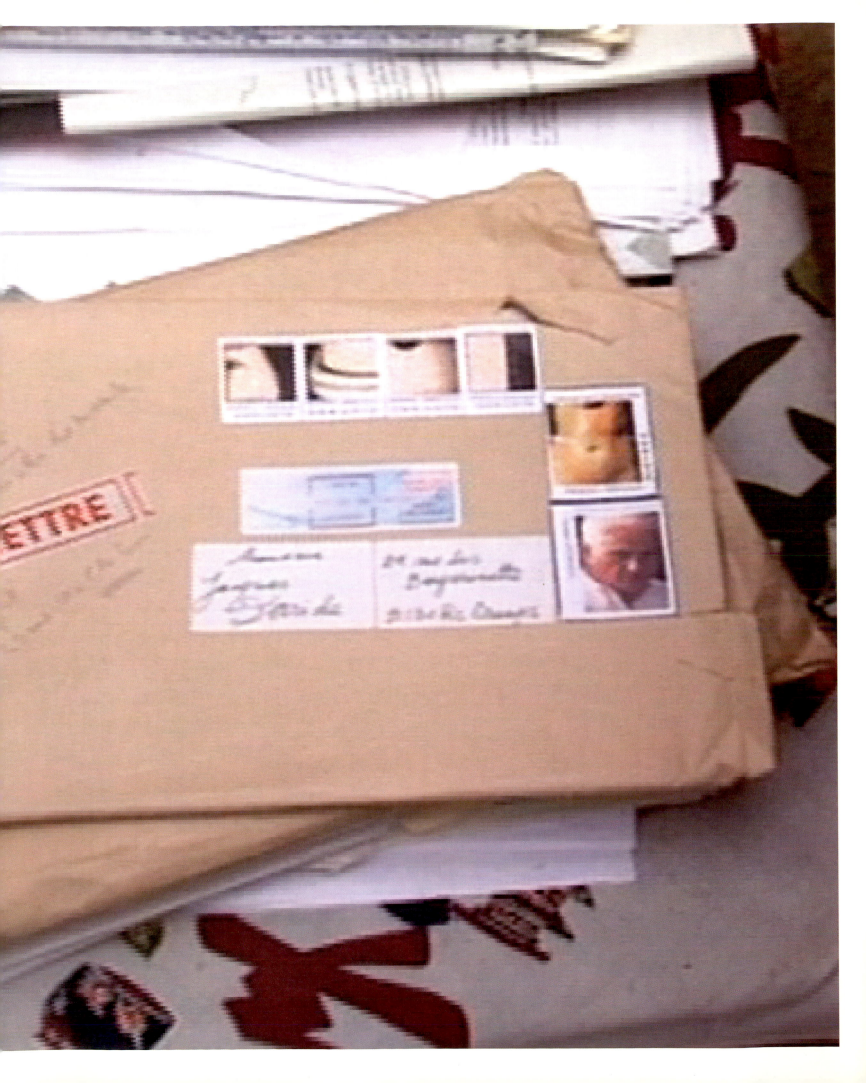

Marianne Macy is a New York based freelance journalist and historian. She interviewed the filmmakers in New York City in October 2002 on the occasion of the film's North American theatrical release.

MARIANNE MACY / KIRBY DICK & AMY ZIERING KOFMAN

Marianne Macy: I'm wondering how the two of you came to work together? Had you known each other, or each other's work, before?

Amy Ziering Kofman: I didn't know Kirby's work at all. We met through a mutual friend who was intent on introducing me to local documentary filmmakers, and then it took about a year from the time of that initial meeting for us to actually decide to work together on Derrida.

MM: Had you, at this point, already received permission from Derrida to do the documentary on him?

AZK: Yes, by the time I met Kirby, I'd already directed a couple film shoots with Derrida.

MM: When Amy first spoke with you about working together on the film, was philosophy something you were interested in and read?

Kirby Dick: I'd read a certain amount. I'd read a great deal of French theory especially Jacques Lacan and some Derrida as well.

MM: Who else? Foucault?

KD: Yes, Foucault. And Deleuze. There was a Deleuze excerpt that I came very close to including in Sick. He'd written a very interesting analysis of sado-masochism. There were a few paragraphs that were very cogent that I'd considered incorporating into the film.

MM: Was this in his "Coldness and Cruelty" essay?

KD: Yes. Exactly. It addressed the humorous situation of a masochist vis-a-vis the law and since Bob was a comedian it was very appropriate.

MM: At that point, when you started working together, did you say to each other, "Let's go after this and this and this" or did the content unfold organically? Did you make an outline or plan?

KD: It was more that we agreed as to what we didn't want. We didn't want to do a primer on his work and we didn't want to make a conventional biopic. We wanted the ambition of his work to provide a challenge for us in terms of our filmmaking and that would incorporate the spirit and thinking of his work without simply explicating it. We were making a film under the influence of his thinking.

MM: Amy, were there things in his writing that you wanted to illustrate?

AZK: Well, yes, maybe not exactly 'illustrate' but in some way respond to or work through. But I didn't start making the film with a clear idea of how I'd accomplish this ambition. It really began to develop once we'd started editing – a process which we only began after we'd completed three or four of the films' major shoots. From this point on though we would always shoot and edit alternately, so that each process informed the other; and we would change, evolve and adapt subsequent work accordingly. Once we saw how one interview worked in the editing process, we would adjust and target the next interview accordingly.

It was never of interest for me to make a film about "who Jacques Derrida is" and present a narrative of his life. For me, the only interest, pleasure and challenge was to make a film that engaged with his work in a way that continually raised the bar for the process of filmmaking and attempted to address the challenge of his work. At best I hoped that the pleasure of reading his text would somehow be reflected in the pleasure of watching the film; but that this filmic translation would not necessitate any reduction of his works' intense complication and richness. I hoped that the film somehow would be equally layered, multi-textural, nuanced and provocative.

MM: Did you speak with Derrida about what you would set out to do?

AZK: No. I gave him a proposal which was sort of a straw dog because whatever you do in a documentary always changes once you begin shooting. I wrote the proposal to get in the door but didn't really have a set idea as to what the film would end up looking like. I knew more what I didn't want it to look like. Jacques continually would ask me questions about the nature and content of the film and I was always pretty vague and evasive. Because for a long time I wasn't really sure what we would end up with but I didn't want him to be concerned. He did not ever offer us any guidance or commentary along the way about what he wanted us to include or do. He was very trusting in that way.

KD: We also looked at a number of attempts by other people to incorporate Derrida's work, not only cinematically but in other mediums, such as art, writing and criticism – works that presented his writing non-academically. One of the limitations with many of these pieces is that often they were so concerned with maintaining a precise consistency with Derrida's work, that they ended up too narrowly constricting their artistic vision. What was intriguing to me about making this film was the impossibility contained within its ambition. How do you present an author's work cinematically? It's a challenge, especially with someone as rigorous and complex as Derrida. Rather than solve the problem by cautiously representing Derrida's work in nearly the same manner that he might present it, we chose to let the difficulty of presenting his work challenge us to develop new forms.

MM: Did you have the idea that the form itself could express the work, say in the way the interviews were edited? For example, did you intend for the way in which Derrida often was or wasn't forthcoming in his responses to somehow illustrate deconstruction?

AZK: Well, we initially did not know that we would use his resistance to our advantage or even that it would figure in the film at all. For a while we found it frustrating but then watching the footage we realized that it was actually sort of interesting in itself and rehearses a sort of commentary in its own right that could be quite productive to work with. So we decided to see what would happen if we started to regard the refusals as a positive thing rather than simply as a shutting down. To repeatedly not say something is in fact to be saying quite a bit, but in a very different way.

KD: Multiple cameras helped us catch these kind of moments which we couldn't have anticipated or really prepared for. We'd quite often used a second, smaller digital camera to shoot Derrida from the moment we'd greet him at the door until the time we'd leave at the end of the shoot. Because this camera seemed almost incidental, he was often much less guarded in front of it, which allowed us to cover his more informal and playful interactions with us.

MM: How did you get all that footage of him at his home in Ris-Orangis outside of Paris?

AZK: About three weeks after Derrida "agreed" to make the film, I got a grant to go to France with a full crew. It came together so quickly that I had very little time to think through what I would do. I told Derrida we would be coming to Paris and ideally would like to film whatever he did. He said, "These are the three days I'll give you and this is what I'm doing this day and that day." It turned out that one of those days he pretty much was just going to be home working and packing in preparation for a trip to the States. Much later in the editing process we decided to use this home footage as a sort of commentary/critique – what does one do with the anecdotal visuals of someone's daily life? What does it tell you, what doesn't it say? To have the seeming banality of the footage comment on our voyeuristic desire to keep looking for something when there is ostensibly nothing there to see. That leads to the issue of biography that the film explores.

KD: This was the first film that was made about Derrida that had a strong focus on his personal life. Now there's no possibility of him ever granting that kind of access again.

MM: Why do you say that?

KD: Well, when someone is making a film about you much of what is shot seems so innocuous, like someone shooting you eating breakfast or listening to the radio. But once you've seen such footage used in a film you realize that it can be very loaded in all sorts of ways you hadn't foreseen, imagined or anticipated.

MM: Like the scene in his kitchen where he's preparing his lunch?

KD: Well that's a good example of how things taken out of context can gain an entirely different valence. Even though that scene was shot eight years ago, because the news on the radio is about an incident in the Middle East, it very well could be describing a more contemporary situation. It's sad to think that this same news still seems current even some five to ten years later. Also, there is this odd quality that this particular piece of news somehow assumes more importance because it's being heard by Derrida (even though he listened to the news daily). Finally, for me, it is reminiscent of the scene at the end of "The Marriage of Maria Braun" by Fassbinder where Hannah Schygulla is in an apartment and a radio is broadcasting the soccer World Cup finals in the 50's that Germany won.

MM: That scene struck me in light of his political activism. Did you intend to have that be an element in the film? Did you think that was important?

AZK: I thought that was very important. My attraction to his work isn't just an idle cerebral exercise. What's always for me been the most significant thing about Derrida's work was its political import. I started reading him before I was taught him in any formal setting and I remember being immediately struck by the strong ethical and political elements in his work. The popular conceptions of deconstruction have been so radically misconstrued by all media that I felt it was important that the film point to his political import but not in a polemical way. Deconstruction is not about nihilism or, as it's often categorized, a relativistic approach such as: "Well, everything is up to interpretation so we can't decide anything." Quite the contrary, the fact that there are competing interpretations makes one more responsible to actively and consciously choose a path and take responsibility for that choice. Not only on paper but throughout his career, Derrida's been an active participant on the forefront of various human rights movements. From apartheid, to public education, to women's rights and the abolition of capital punishment. So, yes, that was very important to me to have in the film.

MM: There seems to be a vein of neurotic, sophomoric knee-jerk type reaction towards him on the part of some of the writers and critics of his work.

AZK: It's baffling to him. It's always been baffling to me. As Derrida says, "If that's what you think then you obviously aren't reading the work," because that isn't what his work is saying at all. On a naïve level all I can guess is that his accusers either: a) don't read the work, so they dismiss it out of ignorance or b) they attempt to read it and find it difficult to understand, and then frustrated and threatened by their inability to understand it, attack it. (Almost as an act of self defense or self ratification – "it must not mean anything because I can't understand it"). But it's really not from any informed place that the critique of deconstruction and Derrida's writing is being made. You may not like it for many reasons but it's not an "anything goes" type of theory at all and it is just silly to attack it as such.

KD: I think on the most basic level the antagonism to Derrida is because of the difficulty of the work. Derrida's work examines how you "get" something, or how you apprehend something, and this examination becomes complicated because he is simultaneously writing about what you are apprehending and how you are apprehending at one and the same time, and that's frustrating for people. On another level, one of the things I found interesting about making this film was that people kept saying, "Isn't he dead?" Obviously it's kind of an antagonistic response, an aggressive response. Amy may not agree....

AZK: Well, I think some of them just really don't know. Didn't you ever say, "Oh, I thought that person was dead?"...

KD: Of course, but I think this phenomenon is a bit more psychological. I've been struck that the name Derrida often prompts a very antagonistic response from people. I actually think in some ways Derrida has had a hand in this. It's a strategy on his part that ...I wouldn't say is premeditated but there's an advantage in having his readership approach him antagonistically. There's more tension in the interaction, and therefore more attention is paid to the work. Someone who approaches Derrida's work from a neutral position may not read the work as closely as someone who is motivated – by an aggressivity that his writing elicits – to look for the flaws in the work. It's a stylistic strategy for him to have his work exist in an arena of antagonism, one that I admire. Many performance artists, Lenny Bruce, for example, use the same strategy. It's not negative. Well, it is negative in a sense but there are real advantages to it. This observation is not in the film but it's something I've thought of a great deal: "Why is there this antagonism towards the name 'Derrida'?"

MM: It's in the nature of his work?

KD: It's aggressive. Very aggressive.

MM: What did Derrida think of the finished film?

AZK: I think he was blown away with what we did the footage. He really had no conception at all throughout the whole process of what we were up to. Having a student write a paper in your seminar about a book by Blanchot is very different from what that student many years later might actually do with footage of you in an on camera interview. I'm just guessing, but I really think he expected something more along the lines of a PBS documentary. From his perspective, we'd done some interviews, we'd filmed in his house, and we'd spoken with him and some of his friends. I think he thought it would just be a nice story about Jacques Derrida and it's not. It's rather a complicated working through of different elements of his own work and his life. I think he was very surprised.

MM: I wanted to ask about the section with his mother, and the visit to the family graveyard in France. How did that come about?

AZK: The idea to use excerpts in this way mostly came from Kirby. I'm very much an academic and I couldn't figure out how to excerpt Derrida's writing. For me it's such a tight and intricate discourse. Everything is so carefully situated and I didn't see how one could successfully extricate a few sentences, but Kirby found some passages that he thought would be particularly effective and started recording these voiceovers where he'd read the passages aloud over selected footage. When we were in Nice interviewing Jacques' siblings, we'd asked Kirsten, our camerawoman, to visit the local cemetery one afternoon and get footage of the family's plots. Kirby then selected a passage from *Circumfession* to read over the footage in the cemetery.

MM: Did you speak to him about that passage or did you just think it was a good illustration?

AZK: Well…no, I didn't (discuss this with him). He's written a great deal about biography and that passage was excerpted from *Circumfession*, a book which itself deals with the insertion of his own biography into a philosophical text, and the dynamic that creates. I was particularly struck by that passage because of the way it continually examines the complexity of the subject's position – as a writer, as a son, as a historical figure, all in a series of developing passages.

MM: Why did the film take so long to make?

AZK: Well, it presented a great number of challenges. For one thing, this film went through many different incarnations because there was no model for how to make it and really no preconceived notion of what the final result might look like. We are thinking of showing on the DVD some examples of the very different editorial approaches we attempted that, for whatever reason, didn't make the final cut. At several points we had a much more abstract film. More like an experimental film, which we pulled back from because we wanted the film to be something that could reach a wide audience and not be just something that might, at best, show in museums on occasion. Likewise I wanted the film to be something that wasn't forbidding or unapproachable, but something that was fun, and that had humor in it. I always think that's effective. Derrida's work has a great deal of humor in it and I felt it was important that the film reflect that as well.

KD: One of the ambitions of this film was to take his work, which in this country is only considered in an academic realm and insert it into a popular medium such as film and then observe what dynamics are created because of that.

MM: Will the rest of your work material join the Derrida archive at the University of California at Irvine, or are there other plans for the material?

AZK: There are two Derrida archives, one in Paris and one at Irvine. Eventually we will archive the footage, but right now we're holding on to everything for the DVD because we'll have to go back to all our source tapes to put that together.

MM: Besides the DVD, is it possible there is enough material for another film?

AZK: Yeah.

KD: Really? (laughs.)

AZK: Well, there's a lot of good footage. Do we have the energy to make another film? That's another question.

MM: You don't have to do it right away.

KD: Actually there is another film that could be made. We did several interviews with Derrida over the course of several years time. Because his answers are so rigorous there're often very lengthy and difficult to incorporate without excerpting and thereby undercutting the entire argument. But an hour long film could be made that includes his more complete answers to certain questions from those four interviews and that could be put together fairly simply and be very interesting.

MM: Did you get to know Derrida well off camera? Was there a different relationship in that circumstance?

AZK: That's an interesting question. No. I actually think the relationship is pretty much the same on and off camera. I think I know him differently but I don't think I know him privately, if that makes sense. That's why I'm reflecting on the answer.

MM: What is the difference?

AZK: Well, in some ways, I know him pretty well. If you go through something like this with someone, you get to know them a lot better than most people. But it's not like we're pals. The way he relates to me…it's not like that. I know him differently than other people but not quite professionally, not quite privately.

MM: How many years was it you worked together?

AZK: I started the project in 1994 and we opened at Sundance in 2002. So I've known him in this capacity for eight years and many years before that I was a student of his.

MM: What was the response like at Sundance?

AZK: Well we finished the film only a day or two before our first screening in Park City and had been clocking insane hours for weeks up until the finish, so we were both in quite an exhausted daze. I remember starting to hear while we were still in LA finishing up the post that our film was one of the first docs to sell out at Sundance – news we found surprising as we hadn't any idea if what we'd found so interesting would be of interest to an audience larger than the small academic circles to which his work's been more conventionally relegated. The film ended up doing very well at Sundance and acquiring something of a 'buzz'. One funny story related to this is that I remember mid week getting a call to the theater asking us if we wouldn't mind holding the film for 10 minutes because "Bob (Robert Redford) was going to come and see it." Sure enough he arrived fifteen minutes later flanked by several bodyguards and proceeded to watch the whole movie. Well, the next day I'm at some event the festival was hosting for the filmmakers and I go up to Geoff Gilmore, the director of the festival, to find out what, if anything, "Bob" might have said to him about our film. And Geoff said, "He told me he liked it, but that he would need to watch it again" and when he said that his bodyguards all unanimously shouted: "NO!"…

MM: So, well, other than the bodyguards, it was well received?

KD: Yes, we did very well at Sundance, and it was pretty much our success with audiences and the press there that led us to get our theatrical distribution deal with Zeitgeist.

MM: This may seem an obvious thought but I'm curious to know if seeing his writing and thoughts on film, or being performed by him was different from the experience of reading them and if this process or experience has in any way changed the writing for you. Did working on the film change or illuminate any of the material or did something jump out at you that might not have before?

AZK: That's an interesting question. If I were to reread his work now, after making the film… I don't think I would interpret it all that differently per se. Working on the film really didn't change that. But when people ask, "What surprised you or what did you learn?" I guess the thing that most surprised me which I couldn't have known, was that Jacques would completely adhere to the ethics that he prescribes in his writing in his relationship to us during the filmmaking project. There was this consistency of rigor – which is something that I'd think would be very hard for a person to successfully sustain over the course of several years in such widely trying and varying circumstances. It was very interesting and surprising to me that there was never any departure from the formal respect that he gives his work. He took all that and extended it to the formal respect he gave the filmmaking process, and exercised all the same care, caution and pedagogical and intellectual integrity. That was surprising.

MM: I wonder if political events now might have added to his scrupulous and unflagging vigilance. There seems to be perhaps more pressure now to look more carefully at meanings, spin, etc.

KD: You mean to have someone be more rigorous about the analysis of rhetoric? Maybe so. Maybe there is such a level of cynicism in the country today - the language has become so Texan, perhaps. We're ready for some continental thinking again.

MM: Towards the end of the film you more directly focus on his archive. Were you attempting to wrap the film up with a consideration of the legacy he's left?

AZK: Derrida's work has always been all about death. The minute he takes up a pen, no matter whatever else he's discussing, he's always in some way preoccupied with the posthumous nature of the act of writing itself – how writing can 'live on' without you being there, you or anyone connected to the ostensibly 'inaugural' act of writing itself. It's a prominent theme in his work, this issue of mortality. Similarly, when you put anyone on film you immediately – whether you intend it or not – become engaged with these types of issues, so we decided to play with that a bit. The film pivots around certain central themes so it was a natural thing for us to include the archive as one of them, and so have some gesture towards a contemplation of mortality and the issues of the archive in our film.

KD: Death inevitably pervades documentary filmmaking and documentary footage. The footage in this film will take on a much different tone and meaning as soon as Derrida dies. For a while during editing I had considered including two minutes of black with no sound near the end of the film. This gap would be prefaced by a card stating that this black section would be replaced by some other footage after Derrida had died. This black would have existed as a memorial to his future death, within the film that we were making while he was alive.

MM: I know Derrida has by now spoken with audiences on at least two occasions after a screening of the film. What's that been like?

KD: Derrida is always great in Q&A's (like the ones he gives after he delivers his lectures) but the Q&A's that have followed after viewings of the film have been somehow different – a bit more unexpected. Obviously, he has to be very affected by seeing himself portrayed in the film, sometimes with many of his friends watching in the audience. It must be somewhat destabilizing emotionally. He's still very witty, charming, and winning, but I've found him to be somewhat more emotional and more personal in the Q&A's after the film. In the Q&A the other night somebody asked him, "Did you fall in love with your wife the first time you met on the trip to the snow?"– a question which he wouldn't answer when we asked it of him in the film. And to my surprise, he quickly responded, "Yes!" I'd fully expected him to avoid answering the question because it was too personal, and instead to spin it into something else. But he didn't. Those moments have been pretty interesting to observe.

MM: So he seems not as controlled or prescribed?

KD: Yes, in a strange way, he's actually very open. And very funny. Although sometimes I think I'm seeing a bit of an act – albeit a very good one. The other night we asked the audience, "Are there any questions?" After a long silence, when no one raised his or her hand, he finally quipped, "It's unquestionable." And of course everyone laughed. Then it occurred to me that he's probably used that line in similar situations many times before.

AZK: Maybe it's a bit like the l'avenir/future schism that Derrida speaks about in the opening of our film, being played out here in a different arena – even what's programmed is always new and what's new can't help but be somehow programmed.

KD: Oh, she always says that…

Credits

DIRECTOR
Kirby Dick
Amy Ziering Kofman

PRODUCER
Amy Ziering Kofman

EDITOR
Kirby Dick
Matt Clarke

MUSIC COMPOSED, PERFORMED,
AND PRODUCED BY
Ryuichi Sakamoto

ASSOCIATE PRODUCER
Gil Kofman

CAMERA
Kirsten Johnson

SECOND CAMERA
Gil Kofman

SOUND
Mark Z. Danielewski
Pascal Depres
Benoit Hillebrandt

STILL PHOTOGRAPHY
Gil Kofman

SUBTITLES
Amy Ziering Kofman

POST PRODUCTION SUPERVISOR
Brian Jonason

ADDITIONAL EDITING
Gil Kofman

FIRST ASSISTANT EDITOR
Brian Jonason

SOUND DESIGN
Mark Korba
Tara Paul

DIALOGUE EDITOR
Dave Scharf

MUSIC MIXED BY
Ryuichi Sakamoto and Fernando Aponte

RECORDED BY
Fernando Aponte

RE-RECORDING MIXER
Mark Linden

TITLES
Mike Kahne

MANAGEMENT FOR RYUICHI SAKAMOTO
KAB America Inc. and KAB Inc. (Japan)
www.sitesakamoto.com

TEXT CITATIONS
Archive Fever
University of Chicago Press, 1996
Mal D'Archive Une Impression Freudienne,
Éditions Galilée, 1995

Circumfession
University of Chicago Press, 1993
Circumfession
Éditions Du Seuil, 1991

Dissemination
University of Chicago Press, 1981
La Dissémination
Éditions Du Seuil, 1972

Ear of The Other
Schocken Books, 1985
L'oreille de L'autre
VLB Éditeur, 1982

The Gift of Death
University of Chicago Press, 1995
Donner la Mort In L'éthique Du Don
Transition, 1992

Memoires for Paul DeMan
Columbia University Press, 1986

Points
Stanford University Press, 1995
Points De Suspension, Entretiens
Éditions GalilÉe, 1992

Writing and Difference
University of Chicago Press, 1967
L'Écriture et La Difference
Éditions Du Seuil, 1967

FOOTAGE AQUISTIONS
'The Late Show'
BBC, 5.13.1992

'Ogrod Sztuk- W Stylu Derridy..Rozmowa Z Filozofem'
TV Polonia, Drecka,, Kamila, 1997

'Sunday Afternoon'
Library Sales, ABC-TV (AUST)

RTBF'S Archives, "Si J'ose Écrire"

KIRBY DICK FILMOGRAPHY

TWIST OF FAITH (2005)
Director
2005 Sundance Film Festival

THE END (2004)
Director

DERRIDA (2002)
Co-Director (with Amy Ziering Kofman)
Golden Gate Award, 2002 San Francisco Film Festival
2002 Sundance Film Festival
2002 Locarno Film Festival

CHAIN CAMERA (2001)
Director
2001 Sundance Film Festival
2001 Edinburgh Film Festival

SICK: THE LIFE & DEATH OF BOB FLANAGAN,
SUPERMASOCHIST (1997)
Director, Producer
Grand Prize, 1997 Los Angeles Independent Film Festival
Special Jury Prize,1997 Sundance Film Festival
Best Documentary Film Nomination, International
Documentary Assoc, 1998
Best Documentary Film Nomination, Independent
Feature Project, 1998

GUY (1996)
Writer
Starring Vincent D'Onfrio, Hope Davis
1996 Venice Film Festival

PRIVATE PRACTICES: THE STORY OF A SEX
SURROGATE (1986)
Director, Producer
Best Documentary,1985 USA Film Festival
Best Documentary, 1985 Atlanta Film Festival

March 20/07